Own Your Greatness

7 Principles To Overcome Tall Poppy Syndrome And Achieve Success

By Mibengé Maria

Copyright

Own Your Greatness: *7 Principles To Overcome Tall Poppy Syndrome And Achieve Success* by Mibengé Maria.

Copyright © 2017 by Mibengé Maria. All rights reserved.

This book or any portion thereof may not be reproduced in any written, electronic, recording, or photocopying form without the express written permission of the author and publisher, except for the use of brief quotations in a book review.

Books may be purchased in quantity and/or special sales via mibengemaria.com or by email at mibengemaria@gmail.com

Printed in Australia

First Printing 2017

ISBN-13: 978-1543280531
ISBN-10: 1543280536
www.mibengemaria.com

To my angels Mariah, Keila and Mayson.

I fell in love with you before you were born and you inspired me to become the greatest version of myself. Thanks to you, I began to trust. Through you, I learned to believe. Because of you, I am able to be. May this book uplift, encourage and validate you for many years to come. Always keep Him first.

CONTENTS

INTRODUCTION	6
CHAPTER ONE	14
CHAPTER TWO	37
CHAPTER THREE	56
CHAPTER FOUR	76
CHAPTER FIVE	93
CHAPTER SIX	110
CHAPTER SEVEN	128
EPILOGUE	145

Acknowledgements

I give all thanks to God, first and foremost. Each day is truly a blessing and I am eternally grateful for this gift called life. A big thank you to my beloved family and friends, you all know who you are.

INTRODUCTION

A wise person once said: *"Treat others as you would like to be treated."* I believe that when you are blessed with profound knowledge and wisdom, you become morally obligated to pay it forward. I have lived by this belief for most of my adult life. Doing so has been rewarding, mentally, physically and spiritually. I began writing this book after realising just how much I have benefited from receiving sound advice from various people over the years. From precious loved ones to complete strangers, people from around the world have shared wisdom with me and I'm eternally grateful. My hope is that by reading this book, you too will acquire new knowledge and wisdom.

The term '*tall poppy*' is defined by the Australian National Dictionary (AND) as: "A person who is conspicuously successful, especially one who attracts envious notice or hostility." Similarly, the Macquarie dictionary describes it as "Someone who is pre-eminent in a particular field; a person with outstanding ability, wealth, or status." It first appeared in Australia in an 1864 Sydney newspaper article which identified tall poppies as those of high rank or status. Though the meaning has shifted over the years, for the purpose of this book tall poppy refers to the above traditional definitions of "high achiever" and "go-getter."

Tall poppy syndrome (TPS) is defined by AND as: "The practice of denigrating prominent or successful people." Tall poppies thrive on ambition, success and possibility — which is not always well received by those who suffer from TPS. Subsequently, tall poppies are often attacked or "cut down to size" in an attempt to "bring them back to reality." We're a society that outwardly roots for the success of others but inwardly anticipates their failure. It is somehow socially acceptable to build people up, only to eventually tear them down. There's a shared belief that you can be successful but not too successful because otherwise your achievements begin to be perceived as arrogance. TPS is a combination of insecurity, envy and schadenfreude. It is highly destructive and ultimately leads to fear of success.

In this book, I share seven ways to finally break free from TPS. I detail how exactly I was able to find the courage to have ambition and to pursue my dreams. I explain how I went from living a life of mediocrity to living a life of greatness in one of the most famous cities in the world. This book is designed to enlighten, inspire and liberate you so that you too can finally begin to live your best life. However, to get maximum value out of this book, you must be truly ready for success. Many people insist they are ready to live a life of greatness, but not many people are ready to do the work. Achieving success in any area of life requires focus and persistence. The difference between those who succeed and those who don't lies in their ability to overcome rejection.

Failure is inevitable but it's how you recover that determines your future.

For years I was lied to by others. I was told I was incapable, unworthy and destined for failure. What's worse is that at one point, I began to believe the lies. Although I had always been raised to value myself, I had never learned how to face rejection. I took every 'no' personally and eventually the rejection broke me. Whether it was naysayers doubting my abilities or not getting my dream job, rejection consumed me. Instead of using it to inspire me to work harder, I began to convince myself that I simply wasn't good enough. By doing this, I subconsciously placed my self-worth in other people's hands and like many often do, I relinquished my power and went into self-destruction mode.

Life is a series of ups and downs and while it may appear easier to stay down and give up, you don't have to. After a few months of self-reflection and self-realisation, I was able to regain my confidence and take my power back. The key in getting back up when you fall lies in letting go of fear. Too many of us use fear as a crutch to make ourselves feel good about choosing a life of mediocrity. We convince ourselves that getting out there and pursuing our dreams is simply 'too hard' and we settle for simplicity. We do this to avoid rejection and anything else that has potential to hurt us. Like a wound that if left untreated causes disease, this type of defence mechanism leads to TPS. When other people are successful, we become uncomfortable mostly because we are reminded that we settled for mediocrity.

Suppressing your skills and talents may make others comfortable, but it is ultimately detrimental to your wellbeing. We are all destined for a life of greatness which can be achieved by fulfilling our life purpose. It's up to each and every one of us to figure out what that is. In this book, we explore unique and effective ways to discover your purpose. We examine internal and external factors that are blocking you from your own success. From toxic relationships to toxic thoughts, this book lists ways that you can change your mind to ultimately change your life.

The most successful people understand the importance of living with intention. This means, having a purpose and fulfilling that purpose every day. Your purpose is your passion and the thing that drives you. Your purpose can often change throughout the course of your life, but you should always be focused and progressing. Without growth, we lose interest so it's important to acknowledge when it's time for change. Regardless of what you believe in from a faith perspective, the universe will always work in your favour. When you have clarity about what it is you want (in love, career, spirituality etc) and if your intentions are good, you are more prone to success.

The secret ingredient in the recipe for success is self-belief. When you believe in yourself, the universe responds by manifesting your thoughts and feelings. This is described as the law of attraction in Rhonda Byrne's best-selling book The Secret. The message of the book is that ultimately, thoughts become things and that we all have the power to create the life we want simply through positive thinking. It's a simple yet powerful concept that has worked for millions of people around the world.

While everyone has the capability to live the life of their dreams, not everyone is focused. We pour our energy into envy and jealousy because we are more focused on other people. Who they are dating, how much money they have, how big their houses are - these are all things that don't concern us. Yet we continue to compare our own lives because too many of us rely on others for validation instead of ourselves. Focusing on other people takes away from our own greatness. Successful people don't worry about others, they stay focused on themselves and expanding their success.

The first step in owning your greatness is to first understand what is working and what isn't. We are often our own worst enemies when it comes to living abundantly. If you don't believe you are worthy of success and happiness, you will never achieve these things. It's important to self-reflect and uncover the blockages. The second step is to retrain your mind and unlearn envy, which is at the root of TPS. It's time to shift your focus from others and put it onto yourself. The third step is to discover your purpose and what it is that motivates you to get out of bed everyday. Self-awareness, honesty and trust are all essential qualities for discovering your true passion in life. Once you have purpose, you begin living with intent.

The fourth step is to take back your power. Too many of us are reliant on those around us to tell us how to live life. By taking control of your life you begin to create the life you want. Life is no longer lived on autopilot and we begin to manifest a life of greatness. The fifth step is one of the hardest — learning to trust yourself. Trust relates to self-acceptance, self-confidence and pride. If you don't like you, no one else will.

Your character, morals and values makeup who we are as people and determine how well we are able to trust ourselves. The sixth step is living with intention. Life without purpose becomes repetitive and dull. Without anything of substance to look forward to, we become disheartened and may even feel a sense of hopelessness. When you discover your passion, you become motivated and excited about each day. The final step is maintaining success, which is vital to avoid falling back into old habits.

In order for change to begin, you have to first believe that it is possible. The key here is to visualise. Imagine how success feels and tastes. Cement this image in your mind and never forget it and sure enough, it will eventually become a reality. As you read this book, continue to have an open mind and open heart and you will be sure to see results. Your life of greatness is just around the corner and now is the perfect time to make it happen.

Own Your Greatness

7 Principles To Overcome Tall Poppy Syndrome And Achieve Success

CHAPTER ONE
Principle 7: Understand envy

If you are not on social media these days, you virtually don't exist. Instagram, Facebook, Twitter and the like have grown more popular in recent years because they are great tools for networking and marketing (among other things). Everyone uses social media for different reasons. Some people use it to showcase their reality, while others use it to escape their reality. With a bit of imagination and the help of advanced apps, you can practically become anyone you want to be online. We all know people who do this. On Snapchat they portray a life of luxury yet in real life, they're struggling to make ends meet. Despite the growing popularity of social media, there are some downsides. For example, various studies have found that some users suffer from a condition called 'social media anxiety depression.'

A 2012 study conducted by the University of Salford and charity group Anxiety UK found that more than half of nearly 300 polled social media users said social media had changed their behaviour. More than half said social media had a negative impact on their behaviour, such as lowered self-confidence. This was mostly due to the tendency to use social media as a tool to compare themselves to others. In 2013, a study by the University of Michigan's psychologist Ethan Kross found that from a poll of roughly 80 Facebook users, most users felt sad or unhappy after using it. Australian teenager Essena O'Neill, a social media influencer who once made thousands of dollars by posting glamorous photos on Instagram, shocked fans in 2015 when she abruptly quit the site claiming it was detrimental - particularly to young women. The 18-year-old, who boasted more than half a million followers, also urged others to follow suit saying:

"I just want younger girls to know this isn't candid life, or cool or inspirational. It's contrived perfection made to get attention."

While some may identify the above studies as proof that social media sites can cause depression and anxiety, others might point out that the sites aren't to blame. Whenever someone posts an achievement online (i.e. showing off a lavish lifestyle), the action of posting itself cannot solely cause anxiety and depression in another person (except maybe in extreme cases). However, generally speaking, a person's relationship with themselves will determine how they react to that post. The same applies in any area of life. One of the most common reactions to other people's success is envy.

There are 3 types of envy according to Australian Psychiatrist Dr. John Buttsworth.

- Knocking people (scapegoating, belittling people)
- Tall poppy syndrome
- Ignoring the success and achievements of others, or exceptional people

Imagine living in a culture where individual success is limited and where excellence is either overlooked or completely ignored. A place where high achievers, with the exception of some sports stars, are resented and attacked. A place where high achievements are discouraged and where finding contentment in mediocrity is highly regarded. Sadly, this is not some fictional tale but rather a cultural phenomenon called tall poppy syndrome (TPS) that exists in some developed nations including Australia, New Zealand and parts of the United Kingdom.

The term "t*all poppy*" was used during the 19th century, as early as 1864 in a Sydney newspaper article about the controversy over the awarding of a knighthood. Since the Commonwealth of Australia was formed in 1901, politicians and other leaders were generally weary about titles and being honoured due to the loyalty many felt to Britain and its customs. Since the First Fleet arrival at Botany Bay in New South Wales on January 18, 1788, British culture has influenced Australian culture. During 1887 Alfred Deakin, who would later become Australia's second Prime Minister and hold the position three times, declined a knighthood offered by the UK government due to concerns about how Australian voters would view him. He instead very modestly opted to be referred to as "mister."

Tall poppy is used to describe high achievers. TPS refers to the glorified culture of criticising, resenting and cutting down tall poppies due to their social status, talents and the very achievements that distinguish them from their peers. It is pack mentality resentment of an accomplished or confident individual, purely out of envy and jealousy. It's the tendency to be critical of anyone deemed by others to be too successful and the process of anticipating their fall and relishing in their decline (schadenfreude). All of this is done with the intention to knock them off their pedestal and "bring them down" a peg or two.

Despite various studies validating the existence of TPS in Australian culture, critics like Liberal Party member Prodos Marinakis call it a myth. In a 1999 written declaration entitled The Black Friday Declaration, the self-described communist-turned-capitalist dismissed TPS as a "destructive myth - which has for decades been promoted by our academics, commentators and journalists." However, researches like Bert Peeters, of The University of Tasmania, suggest otherwise. He studied TPS in Australia and shared his findings in his 2004 paper *Tall poppies and Egalitarianism in Australian discourse*. In it, the social phenomenon is described as the *'widespread tendency... to scrutinise high achievers and cut down the tall poppies among them.'*

Some critics argue that TPS extends beyond Australia, New Zealand and the UK and in fact, the term was once alluded to by former American steel company executive, Benjamin Franklin Fairless. While speaking at a government hearing on Study of Monopoly Power in 1950, the late American businessman said:

"We believe that there is one economic lesson which our twentieth century experience has demonstrated conclusively —that America can no more survive and grow without big business than it can survive and grow without small business.... the two are interdependent. You cannot strengthen one by weakening the other, and you cannot add to the stature of a dwarf by cutting off the legs of a giant."

Throughout history, America, unlike Australia, has managed to avoid the trap of TPS and prides itself on being the "land of opportunity." This is prevalent when you consider the American Dream, which is a set of ideals based on the common understanding that through honest hard work, success is attainable. In American culture, individualism and freedom to reach your full potential is celebrated and experts say upward socio-economic mobility is accessible to everyone.

The late Dame Nellie Melba (born Helen Porter) was among the first to experience TPS in Australia during the late 1800s. Her many achievements as an opera singer, included becoming the first Australian to be internationally recognised for her singing in New York and parts of Europe. She was also hailed for her charity work during World War I and became the first Australian to cover Time magazine in 1927. Despite her feats, she was often subject to unsubstantiated reports by the media about heavy drinking, drug use and promiscuity — which at times overshadowed her work.

In 2012, acclaimed actress Melissa George, who like many other Aussie stars moved abroad early in her career to achieve mainstream success, said TPS is the reason many leave. She was accused of being a 'diva' by the press after raising concerns about questions she was asked during a TV interview. She said they completely disregarded her achievements by focusing on the show which had launched her career years prior. She vented on Twitter and later apologised for her tweets.

'It's 20 years ago. I always embrace the past, am used to being misquoted, and love my fans, but the tall poppy syndrome is pushing us away.

I'd rather be having a croissant in Paris or walking my French bulldog in New York City. I'm not going to be a good Aussie anymore.

I'm going to speak out. I've just had it. It's disgusting. I've never spoken out about it because I have to be the loyal good Aussie who goes away and comes home but I'm really hard-working and people have to respect me for what I've done.'

More recently, Sydney-born Rebel Wilson also called out Australian media for its TPS culture. She was raised in west Sydney, has a law degree, starred in multiple Hollywood blockbusters and has numerous TV and film accolades. In 2015, years of hard work became completely overshadowed by media reports that she lied about her age.

A gossip magazine quoted a "former high school friend" as saying Wilson was much older than she had claimed and that despite the actress portraying a humble upbringing, she grew up in an "upper-middle-class" family. The report went viral and while the American media was mostly forgiving, back in her native of Australia, backlash ensued. Some critics called the incident a classic case of envy. In a tweet, Wilson laughed off the controversy and later attributed misrepresenting her age to sexism and ageism in Hollywood.

'OMG I'm actually a 100 year old mermaid formerly known as "CC Chalice" ....thanks shady Australian press for your tall poppy syndrome x.'

She later sued Bauer Media for defamation and in 2017, was awarded Australia's highest ever defamation payout of $4.5 million.

In 2015, singer Nikki Webster recalled how TPS became so overwhelming that it drove her out of Australia. She rose to stardom in 2000, as the 13-year-old star of the Sydney Olympics opening ceremony after being plucked from 500 hopefuls. Despite capturing hearts around the world with her magnetic performance, she said the reception back at home was "dark" thanks to TPS. She was left devastated because as she described, she became "the punchline of everyone's joke."

In an interview with *The Daily Telegraph* she said:

"I was just this young naive artist trying to make a go and work hard. I'd worked damn hard and I wasn't getting the reception, I couldn't understand it."

TPS extends beyond the entertainment sector. In 2014, Matt Hutchinson, a two-time Young South Australian of the Year and orthopaedic surgeon recalled how TPS forced him to retreat from public life. He was once elected president of the Australian Medical Students' Association and was passionate about finding new ways to help those less fortunate.

The once outgoing humanitarian was left devastated and withdrawn after media outlets began to question his achievements. For years, the father-of-two had been honoured for his international charity work and leadership role as a medical student, but one day an anonymous email sent to the media threatened to undo all of his hard work. Years prior, he admittedly broke a no-alcohol rule during a uni football trip. While he was eventually cleared of wrongdoing, following an internal investigation by the University of Adelaide, the media backlash changed him forever.

In an interview with News Corp he said:

"I just went to ground; I got a bit paranoid that people were trying to tear me down. I wonder how many young people go through something similar — does a pretty hard-edged Aussie society chop down lots of young people, and stifle what could have been very creative and much-needed leadership and fresh ideas?"

Australia is commonly referred to as the "lucky country" because it is often viewed as being the land of equal opportunity, where anyone and everyone can live freely and comfortably. Culturally, it prides itself as being an egalitarian nation, meaning it values equal rights and equal possibility for all. Our traditional underdog culture is a key attribute that sets us apart from other developed nations and it is also what undoubtedly makes us so likeable around the world. We are a nation where, as some cultural experts have previously stated; *"no-one is left behind."* Our trademark *"fair-go"* mentality and *"on-ya mate"* attitude distinguishes us in the western world as being a respected nation of great honour and humility.

While for decades, Australia has thrived on the global playing field as an industrialised nation, therein lies a problem with its highly valued egalitarian culture. In his 1964 book *The Lucky Country*, Australian professor Donald Horne takes a critical look at 1960s Australia, particularly its economic prosperity. He argues that during that time, the nation's wealth was heavily reliant on natural resources in contrast with other developed nations — which were prospering through creative innovations like technology and original ideas.

He states: '*Australia is a lucky country run mainly by second rate people who share its luck. It lives on other people's ideas, and, although its ordinary people are adaptable, most of its leaders (in all fields) so lack curiosity about the events that surround them that they are often taken by surprise.*'

It could be argued that this same lack of innovation that Horne describes in his book, is a direct implication of the nation's egalitarian and underdog cultures. The common belief that everyone is equal in political, economic and social status, though beneficial because it fosters the notion of equal opportunity, can also be counterproductive in that it fails to properly recognise high achievers which can lead to TPS. While some sociologists argue that TPS is on the decline throughout Australia, it is still very much prevalent within our culture today and is far more detrimental than people realise because ultimately it can harm the economy and hinder our overall potential as a nation. The biggest problem with TPS is that it perpetuates the myth that in order for success to be maintained, it must be capped or limited. This false theory can create an overwhelming fear of success.

The idea that one is allowed to be great but not too great, is a flawed way of thinking because it legitimises the fear of one's own greatness and encourages internal doubt which often results in finding contentment in mediocrity. It causes us to suppress our skills and abandon our creative talents so that we "blend in" with the average Joe to make others more comfortable. We begin to downplay or even reject our unique abilities and ignore our full potential in a bid to be socially accepted, respected and liked.

With this mentality, striving for excellence and a life of greatness makes others uncomfortable and therefore one is encouraged to opt for status quo to "keep the peace." Some critics say Australia is a nation of haters who build people up only to tear them down. After all, we have a strange habit of rooting for the underdog or underachiever but once they reach a certain level of success, we start to resent them and cut them down. We start to believe that the tall poppy's triumph and success translates to our own failings, which leads to a self-created inferiority complex.

In the 1980s, Australian social psychologist Norman Feather led research at The Flinders University of South Australia which analysed tall poppies and schadenfreude in Australia. Feather conducted three separate studies in his 1989 paper *Attitudes Toward the High Achiever: The Fall of The Tall Poppy.* One particular study asked high school students to respond to scenarios in which either a high achiever and an average achiever experienced failure. Not surprisingly, results showed subjects were most satisfied seeing the high achiever fail as opposed to witnessing the average achiever fail.

It is understandable that a sports nations like Australia would idolise sports stars but why does this type of praise not extend outside of sport and into other sectors — business, education, politics and the arts? In America, people of genuine merit and high achievements are generally honoured and celebrated. This recognition propels messages of hope and possibility which then inspires others in their personal journeys.

Rags-to-riches stories are admired and often set the bar for others also striving for excellence and greatness. This is not the case is Australia. While Aussies may at times be encouraged to pursue success, we fail to acknowledge it when it is in fact achieved. This mindset is damaging and ultimately harmful to the nation's economy because as any wise person knows, as times change it's time to be proactive or adapt.

As women and other minorities continue to fight for equality in Australia, for rights such as equal pay, it is safe to say that we have come a very long way. Let's take a moment to acknowledge just how far we have come. For decades, Australia has been a global leader in recognising the need for gender equality and taking necessary measures to enforce this right. In 1902 Australia became the second country in the world to grant women the right to vote and it was also the first nation to give women the right to stand for election in federal parliament. In 2013 we elected our first ever female prime minister and more than ever women around the nation are being employed in leadership roles and making use of existing equal rights.

Women are realising more than ever that they are far more than just a pretty face. Yes, we are indeed nurturers, mothers, grandmothers, sisters, daughters, aunts, wives and girlfriends but we are also capable of being much more. More Australian women are striving to become entrepreneurs, leaders, pioneers and CEOs so we must make the necessary societal changes to ensure that they are given the best possible shot at pursuing their dreams.

In this book, you will learn how to finally break-free from TPS to live the life of your dreams.

Take action:

Identify. Release. Renew.

A wise person once said, *"you are who you hang with."* This saying has been scientifically proven time and time again, which is why you should always be conscious of your surroundings and who you allow into your space. A 2014 study by researchers at the Max Planck Institute for Cognitive and Brain Sciences and the Technische Universität Dresden in Germany found that stress is contagious, meaning that it has the ability to "rub off" on others. The study involved more than 100 pairs made up of strangers and loved ones. One person observed the other enduring stressful situations (i.e. completing arithmetic and being interviewed) through a one-way mirror or live video feed.

Not surprisingly, the majority of those placed under direct stress showed signs of stress. What was fascinating was that 26 percent of observers (or those watching the stressful situations) had increases in their levels of the stress hormone cortisol. The increase in stress levels was particularly high among the observers watching loved ones (or someone they knew), with 40 percent becoming stressed compared with only 10 percent of observes watching strangers. It is common knowledge that there are often health risks associated with stress. From weight problems to battling depression, stress can pose both physical and emotional health issues and in some instances it can lead to fatal diseases like cancer.

We will all experience stress at some point in our lives and though it can be difficult, it is a relatively normal part of life. It is how you react to problems like stress that truly matters. How you approach your perceived problems ultimately determines the direction of your future. Everything is cause and effect. Your reaction has the power to either pull you out of darkness (i.e. stop feeling envious of others) or heighten your misery (i.e. manifest envy). Happiness is a personal choice and choosing to have a positive mindset goes a very long way. Whether you view the glass as being half empty or half full is your choice and your choices are constantly manifesting and shaping your future.

Thoughts become things so it is vital to your wellbeing that you make a conscious effort each day to fill your mind with positive thoughts. Surrounding yourself with positive people and positive energy is imperative on your quest for greatness. Those who do not fit this mould will only hinder your growth and distract you from living the life you truly deserve. You need to eliminate all sources of toxicity if you truly want to live your best life and become the person you were destined to be. People who suffer from TPS fail to realise this and often thrive on negativity which is a very dangerous and destructive way to live. Some examples of sources of toxicity include:

- People (negative friends, lovers, or family members)
- Unhealthy habits (smoking, excessive eating)
- Work (soul-destroying job or dead-end career)

For many people, family is the most important thing in life. However, sometimes those closest to us or those we love most are the most common sources of toxicity. Whether consciously or subconsciously, family, friends or lovers can sometimes hinder you the most from progressing. If they have negative views on life and negative ways of thinking, there is a chance they might pass that on to you - no matter how strong-minded you may be. This is not to suggest that you should abandon negative people. However, in order for you to get the most out of this book you will need to be open to making drastic life changes. Depending on your situation, this means reassessing your social circles and loving people from a distance until you have completed this book.

Ask yourself the following questions:
- Who are the people I spend most of my time with?
- How do they generally feel about themselves?
- Do they radiate positive energy and engage in uplifting conversations on a regular basis?
- Do they make me feel uplifted and happy?

When I was 16 and at high school, I had an epiphany about friendships. I had this profound realisation after having spent countless years striving to be popular and gain approval from others. I suddenly learned not to care what others think and to focus on quality not quantity in my friendships. I realised by observing others that "popular" and "cool" are meaningless and ultimately illusions. Through my own heartbreak and disappointment, I realised that there is great value in being selective about your social circle. So I began closely reassessing my friendships to ensure that I was around the right people. As I began eliminating certain people, I began to evolve and felt happier than ever.

Remove all sources of negativity in your life, starting with the people you allow in your space. After reassessing your social circle, consider other external factors that have the power to influence your thoughts, mood and ideas. Everything from what you read first thing in the morning to who you phone chat with before bed each night, should be carefully considered.

Do the people who you spend most of your time with leave you feeling uplifted and happy or drained and miserable? Reading beauty magazines every morning is likely to leave you feeling inadequate and insecure, just as spending time with the office gossip at work is likely to spark mean-spirited conversation and ultimately trigger negative thoughts. The same could be said about chatting on the phone to a depressed friend every night. It will almost always leave you feeling downcast and gloomy. Where energy goes, intention flows. Be aware of your surroundings at all times and who you allow into your sacred space.

As the saying goes; *you will never soar with the Eagles while hanging around Turkeys.* Sacrifice will play a pivotal role in how much you get out of this book. You must be open to eliminating toxicity to overcome TPS and live your best life. If you are not open to change, this book will be of no use to you. Gossips, backstabbers, liars, mean girls, naggers and complainers are further examples of toxicity. They will only block your ability to succeed in life. It's important to allow yourself to release all negative energy from your life. Again I repeat, this book will be of no use to you unless you genuinely want meaningful change in your life.

As you continue reading this book, you will notice my love of famous quotes. Reading powerful quotes has helped me throughout my journey and one of my all-time favourites is:

"A comfort zone is a beautiful place, but nothing ever grows there." - Anon.

RECAP

In Chapter One, we defined envy and TPS. Envy is a natural emotion that every human feels at some point. However, rather than feed into it, learn to channel your emotions by focusing on the positive. The power of positive thinking goes a very long way. For example:

Negative thought: *Her life looks so glamorous, why can't I have her life?*
Positive thought: *Her life looks so glamorous, her success is proof that I too can achieve that.* A simple shift in the way you think, will have a tremendous impact on your overall state of mind. You cannot control your thoughts and emotions, but you can always channel your energy into something constructive. Allow yourself to feel each and every emotion but remember to release it when it no longer serves you.

We also explored sources of toxicity and the importance of carefully selecting who and what you allow into your space. Your focus should now be on these three important steps: Identify, Release, Renew.

- Identify: It is impossible to ever make any life changes without first identifying the problem. What is the source of the negative energy in your life? Is it certain people? Your job? Your lifestyle? Your beliefs? Bad habits? You should closely consider your situation and whether it brings you joy and contentment. Do you wake up every morning feeling content and fulfilled? Do you go to bed every night feeling happy? Do you generally feel great and excited about life? Write down all the things that are causing your unhappiness. Then be open to letting them all go.

- Release: After identifying the sources of toxicity, find the courage and willpower to eliminate this from your life. This could mean anything from cutting out junk food to ending a toxic relationship. Perhaps it's a combination of things? Whatever the case, you need to let it go now. I cannot stress enough how pertinent this is to your personal growth. Be willing and open to finding your inner strength and letting go of whatever no longer serves you.This will be easy for some and difficult for others but it must be done to create change.

- Renew: *"We cannot solve our problems with the same thinking we used when we created them" - Albert Einstein.*
Eliminating toxicity requires a maintenance plan to prevent you from returning to old habits. You must shift your thinking and alter your mindset. Knowing something is bad for you is not the same as knowing why it is bad for you. In fact, I don't believe that it is possible to permanently release something that is

harmful to you without fully understanding why it is harmful to you.

For example, dumping your boyfriend because your Mother tells you he is bad for you is one thing, while dumping him because you accept that he is abusive towards you is another. Being told that something is wrong and understanding that something is wrong are very different. You should know why something is bad for you before you can release it from your life, if you are serious about meaningful change. Otherwise you run the risk of it returning and going back to square one. You often see this played out with couples who are always on and off. They generally know that they are toxic for each other but may not actually understand why. When you don't understand, you cannot make informed decisions. You need to renew your outlook and change your perspective by taking a close look at your situation from a bird's-eye view. Analyse and assess. If need be, write down a list of pros and cons for each perceived problem. The sooner you understand why something is toxic, the sooner you can release it from your life for good.

NOTES

CHAPTER TWO
Principle 6: Unlearn envy

From a young age, we're conditioned to conform and be like everyone else. This is usually learned at school. From wearing a uniform to following the rules, you learn that it is "right" to follow the majority. In fact, anytime someone dares to even slightly veer off course or challenge the system by doing their own thing, they are deemed rebels and punished. You are conditioned to believe that in order to fit in and be accepted, you should be like the majority.

And as you get older, it's much of the same. You are taught to chase the Australian dream which means going to school, getting a job, buying a house (with a white picket fence of course), getting married, having kids and living happily ever after. But this rigid life plan is a lie. While it may have worked for some in the 1950s, life is far more complex today. To truly live a life of freedom and happiness, you will need to unlearn much of what you were taught and retrain your mind. And more people are slowly beginning to realise this.

More than ever before, people are becoming conscious and more curious about the earth and human existence. Thanks in-part to the digital age, we have access to more information, more ideas, more opportunities and more options than ever before. Humanity is evolving and more and more people are realising that while living a life of mediocrity is comfortable, we all have so much more to offer the world.

With more people tapping into this new energy of consciousness and awareness and new ways of living, the Australian dream (in a traditional sense) has evolved, much like society. We want to progress and we want more out of life. More of us want to travel, live abroad, learn about new cultures, fight for equality, rescue animals, start businesses, freeze our eggs, protect the environment and even end world poverty. And in order for us to fulfil our dreams, we must be willing to honour our own skills and talents. Change is a perfectly natural and healthy part of life, so why does it make others uncomfortable? The answer is simple — because we're conditioned to be like everyone else. So when people or the environment around us changes, our own identity is called into question.

Where do I fit into all of this change? Am I still valuable? If my neighbour progresses, where does that leave me?

For too long, we have been taught to be like others and strive for simplicity to achieve happiness. Remember the conditioning: school-work-house-marriage-kids-retirement. This is a lie. While it may have worked for our parents, it no longer works in today's society. We want more. While not everyone is born to be a doctor or an astronaut, we all have individual skills and talents that make us unique and great in different ways. But while everyone *should* be utilising their skills and talents, and living their best life, most people are not.

Yes, working a 9-5 job you don't love and living a quiet life in the suburbs might appeal to you, but *are you truly content and happy? Do you truly believe that you are honouring your full potential and living you best life?* If the answer is yes, then you may as well put this book down now because it will be of no use to you. But chances are that you picked up this book for a reason, which is that you are finally ready for meaningful change in your life. You are certainly not alone. More and more people are fed up with the rigid life plan they were conditioned to believe in. Maybe you are tired of working long hours at a dead-end job just to pay bills? Or you are tired of feeling stuck in a marriage or relationship that you feel is blocking you from your own success? Maybe you simply don't have the energy to change whatever it is you need to change? Well, you've already taken the first step to investing in yourself, which shows you are ready and serious about finally achieving true happiness.

We have more leaders, entrepreneurs and business owners in the world today than ever before. More people want to progress and are tapping into their own unique skills and talents to live their best life, but some people object to this. As tall poppies achieve success, others try to cut them down. We all witness this on a daily basis. High achievers who are resented because of their own success. Whether it's the guy down the street who drives the latest luxury car or a friend who just bought a lavish home — their achievements upset others. But why? Surely when someone is rewarded for honest, hard work they should be celebrated and not resented by their peers? Why are high achievers suddenly resented once they reach success? The answer is envy and jealousy. As a tall poppy grows, their achievements leave others feeling insecure and unsure about themselves — again, because we're taught to be like everyone else. We begin to ask ourselves: *If they're achieving success, where does that leave me?* A wise person once said *"comparison is the thief of joy,"* yet many continue to compare their lives with others. The simple solution to this is stop comparing. Instead, learn to channel that energy into your own success. You can do this by understanding three key points:

- Your envy comes from a place of lack:
  The reason that you envy others is because you don't feel good enough as you are. You are not happy and content

with your life so it makes you uncomfortable to see others enjoying success. You are not honouring your skills and talents and might even suppress your true potential to make others feel comfortable. At some point in your life, you consciously or subconsciously chose to live a life of mediocrity, so seeing others excel is a painful reminder of that choice. No-one wants to live a mediocre life yet you chose to do so because it probably felt comfortable. Whether it's the career you chose, the spouse you chose, the house you chose — you aren't content and will never truly be happy until you break-free from the pattern and mental conditioning.

- Their success does not result in your failure:
  As Tall poppies achieve success, others will fall victim to Crab mentality. This means cutting them down and sabotaging their success out of fear of not achieving the same success. If I can't achieve it, no-one can — this way of thinking is detrimental to all involved. Stop comparing yourself to others. The reason you will never be content with where you are in life and what you have is because you continue to compare yourself. Where energy goes, intention flows. Instead of envying others, take time to discover and honour your own greatness.

If someone is enjoying success in their business, that does not make you a failure for not being a business owner. If someone loses lots of weight and looks great, that doesn't make you a failure for not having lost the same weight. If someone meets and marries the love of their life, that doesn't make you a failure for being single. What's worse than envying others is trying to somehow justify that envy. You will often hear envious people speak negatively about those they envy to feel better about themselves. *Business is going well for him, but he's become so arrogant. She's lost so much weight, but she's so full of herself now. Now that she's found love, she's not as good a friend as she used to be.* Even if there was truth to any of your negative thoughts, complaining will not improve your situation. By feeding into negative thoughts, you manifest negativity in your life. Instead, learn to use the success of others as your inspiration. It's time to take responsibility for your life. Stop blaming others and start investing time and energy into your success.

- Honour your greatness:
  TPS is learned behaviour. We have been taught from a young age to suppress our excellence to make others comfortable. You can strive for success, but not be too great. This is a lie. Suppressing your skills and talents is detrimental. You weren't born to pay bills and die. You weren't born to live a boring life of mediocrity. You were born to live your absolute best life. Take a few minutes to think in silence about the following questions before answering them. What are you passionate about? What fires you up and makes you want to take action? What

makes you happy?

If you answered these questions honestly and seriously, the answer indicates your life purpose. Now ask yourself this, are you living out your life purpose? Chances are you are not otherwise you probably wouldn't have picked up this book. Your time is now. It's time to get serious about your greatness and your happiness. There is no room for excuses. Having children is not an excuse. Having a demanding job is not an excuse. You can make time for yourself. Even just 15 minutes a day is enough time to brainstorm some of those amazing ideas you have. Start investing in YOU. Believe that you are worthy of happiness and get to work. No-one can transform your life but you. There is no magic wand to begin living a life of greatness. It all starts with you.

Take action:

Envision. Believe. Trust.

With anything in life, you have to be the change that you want to see. Now that you have cleaned up your external surroundings (Chapter One), it's time for your internal cleanse. Here, we will awaken the mind, body and spirit and ensure that they are all in synch. This will help you discover your true self and live your best life. How you feel about yourself internally is often reflected externally. This book is designed to transform you from the inside out, but in order for you to get the most value, you should believe that change is possible and that you are worthy of greatness.

In 2010, shortly after graduating from university I packed up my bags and moved to New York City to pursue my dreams of becoming a journalist. Before my big move, I first had to wholeheartedly believe that my dream was even possible. Success was not guaranteed but I genuinely believed in myself, so I made it happen. I did not have a job, accommodation or friends but I believed in my own potential. Naturally, there was a cloud of doubt which sat in the back of my mind, but I learned to quiet this negative voice by embracing my inner optimist. I had big dreams and I could not afford to relinquish my inner power to naysayers. I began planning and I made a daily habit of envisioning my New York dream. I fantasised about my success and how it felt, smelt and tasted. I pictured myself interviewing some of the biggest stars in Hollywood on some of the most prestigious red carpets.

For months, I envisioned, believed and trusted in my dream and eventually it became a reality. The process was difficult and required internal reflection and drastic change. I first had to accept that the person I was, was not the same person I envisioned myself becoming. I was a person who found contentment in comfort, routine and fear. I was a people pleaser, who constantly sought validation from others. I could no longer continue as I was, if I truly wanted to live a life of greatness. Something had to change. I had to drastically shift my thinking and change my mindset to become the fearless go-getter I envisioned in my dreams.

MIND

In Chapter One we looked at the power of positive thinking, which relates to mind. What we think about, we bring about. A negative mind will almost always produce negative results, which is why it is crucial that you let go of old thought patterns. People suffering from TPS try to normalise envy and judgmental thoughts by masking it as simply observing flaws in other people. This is a lie and a detrimental way of thinking. Putting down others and finding flaws in everyone but yourself is unhealthy and self-destructive. Learn to shift the focus from other people to your own life. Replace every negative thought with a positive and watch the magic unfold.

By now, you should have gained some clarity as to what you want to achieve from this book. I encourage you to write down all of your life goals. Do you dream of being a home owner? Perhaps you've always wanted to be a fashion designer? Whatever it is that you dream of and that makes you excited about life, is what you should pursue. Your life goals, which by the way will naturally change throughout your journey, should be clear and realistic. Clarity is key. I repeat. Clarity is key. If you aren't clear about what you want, you will never get clear results. You should be very honest with yourself. While dreaming big is great, unless you are realistic about your life goals, you will be forever chasing them. Aspiring to make it as a high fashion runway model when you are 4 feet tall, curvy and approaching age 50 is unrealistic. Once you have established attainable goals that are bound with good intentions, anything is possible.

The information that we consume on a daily basis has a tremendous impact on our psyche. Closely consider the information that you are taking in on a daily basis. Is the content positive and constructive? Negative content will almost always provoke negative thoughts and feelings. For example, while watching fights on TV might be entertaining for some, for others however, the violent content might spark feelings of rage — ultimately triggering strong emotions. In contrast, reading a beautiful poem or a romance novel is more likely to promote peace and calmness.

Pay attention to the content you consume. As a journalist, I can attest to the fact that some media outlets have an agenda. In a world of fake news, people try to have you believe things that aren't necessarily true as part of that agenda. One important source of information in the digital age is social media, which many people around the world enjoy. By the end of 2016, Facebook had 1.8 billion users worldwide. While they can be wonderful tools for networking, most of what you see in your feed or timeline is someone else's highlight reel. You will sometimes see a warped and exaggerated version of someone else's reality which can trigger feelings of envy. Resist the urge to compare yourself with others. Too many of us fall into the trap of comparing ourselves with one another. Competing with others on social media for validation is about as useful as internet trolling. Jealously and envy are natural emotions. Learn to channel your emotions into something constructive. If engaging in social media doesn't leave you feeling uplifted and happy, then you might want to rethink using it. Fill your heart and mind with positive thoughts and constructive material and watch your life change for the better.

A wise person once said:

"You are today where your thoughts have brought you, you will be tomorrow where your thoughts take you." - James Lane Allen.

It took me years to master the art of positive thinking. After a difficult childhood and some personal set backs in my teen years, I became bitter and irrational. Years of hurt, disappointment and mistreatment left me broken and rebellious during my teenage years and it was at that point in my life that I decided people could not be trusted.

I decided that all women were backstabbers and that all men were jerks. I gave into fear and frustration. Although it took me years to realise, I now accept that my generalisations and assumptions were complete lies. It was while reading books like *The Law of Attraction* (Esther and Jerry Hicks), *The Art of Happiness* (by the Dalai Lama and Howard Cutler) *and The Power of Now* (Eckhart Tolle), in my 20s that I learned about positive thinking and the law of attraction. Both foster the notion of "like attracts like." Instead of waking up every morning dreading my long day at work or at uni, I began practicing gratitude.

Waking up grateful each morning would set the tone for my day. Instead of waking up annoyed, envious of others and hung-up on my past, I channelled my emotions by accepting what I couldn't change, to appreciate everything that was good in my life.

BODY

The first step in the body renewal process is to take a close look at your diet and lifestyle routine. Do you regularly monitor the food that you eat? Do you exercise? Do you get adequate sleep? I have always tried my best to lead a healthy lifestyle but there's always room for improvement. After graduating from uni, I decided to improve my lifestyle so that I could truly look and feel my best. This included cleaning up my eating pattern and adopting an exercise routine. My changes were not too drastic and I refused to deprive myself of anything, but that small change was still effective.

Something as minor as changing what I ate for breakfast each morning (I swapped bacon and eggs for healthier options like fruit and oatmeal) not only helped me lose weight but also gave me loads of energy. In addition to the dietary changes, I committed to more regular workouts. I made a conscious effort exercise daily for even if only for 20 minutes.

As previously mentioned, how you feel on the inside almost always reflects on the outside which is why it is paramount that you make a conscious effort every single day to protect your mind, body and spirit. When these three elements are in synch, a reawakening process begins and your life is lived more consciously.

New York is among a growing number of cities around the world that are beginning to promote conscious living. Each and every day on the streets of Manhattan you see communities uniting for a good cause. The city is filled with libraries, gyms, yoga studios, vegan restaurants, juice lounges, charities, churches and prayer rooms. New Yorkers understand the value in balancing mind, body and spirit and using it as a basis for personal development and inner growth.

Body renewal tips:

- Healthy eating: At least one piece of fruit daily, colourful foods, portion control, plenty of water.
- Regular exercise: Any daily physical activity that increases your heart rate is great. Be consistent with workouts, go on regular walks, challenge yourself.
- Eliminate the toxins: Avoid drugs, alcohol and risqué behaviour.

Nourish your body with nutritious foods, make exercise a priority and stimulate your mind with positive content — then watch your life change drastically. Not only will you improve your health and boost your energy levels, but you will also begin to exude confidence and inner happiness. I highly recommend a short-term fast or bodily cleanse for a week to renew your. Doing this will eliminate toxins and shock your body enough to reap maximum benefits from your new lifestyle.

SPIRIT

The final part of this three-piece equation is spirit which, depending on what you believe, is at the core of who we are as human beings. We are more than flesh and far greater than what meets the eye. Our potential knows no bounds and our abilities are endless. To tap into your highest power, you will need to develop your spirituality (if you haven't already). It is important to note that the word *spirituality* means different things to different people. While some associate it with religion, for others it can mean meditation, yoga or nature.

You should believe in something greater than yourself. Whether this is the universe, God or something else, what you believe in is your personal choice. This is to instil faith, which in essence instills hope. You cannot achieve anything in life without any hope. You cannot have any hope without belief. Believing in something gives us a sense of life and purpose. Just as food nourishes the body, spirituality nourishes the soul and therefore it is essential that you believe in something greater than yourself.

Religion is a very broad and complex topic that I think everyone should take the time research independently at some point. Doing your own due diligence gives you the ability to make informed decisions as it relates to you and your beliefs. Once you grasp the importance of protecting your mind, body and spirit, your life will instantly improve for the better.

RECAP

Envision: Clarity is key. You will need to establish your goals and what it is that you want out of life to initiate any form of change. If you are not clear about what kind of life you want to live, you will never progress. Too many people make the mistake of "going with the flow" and doing just enough to get by in life, because it's comfortable. If this is you and you have no desire to change your life, this book will be of no use to you. Living a life of mediocrity should not be an option for anyone, so it's time to discover your passion in life. Envisioning your life goals is not always easy so be sure to take your time with this process. If need be, go somewhere quiet and place your hand on your heart and ask yourself what it is that your heart desires. The answer should be given almost immediately. Another option is to meditate and connect with source, which is effective in gaining clarity.

Believe: If you don't believe in you, no-one else will. This is a fact. When you have clarity about life, you will naturally feel passionate about everything that you do. An internal cleanse will eliminate toxicity to give you clarity about what it is that you want out of life. When the mind, body and spirit are in synch, life flows beautifully and believing in yourself becomes second nature. Your goals should stem from good intentions.

Think about what it is that you want. What is your long-term goal? Will your goal benefit others? For example: aspiring to be rich for material purposes and to show off to others is a goal that stems from bad intentions and lacks substance. As best-selling author Rick Warren once told me (quoting another writer) at an awards show in Nashville: *"We buy things we don't need, with money we don't have to impress people we don't even like."* Clarity and intention are key in achieving anything.

Trust: Trust that anything is possible and believe in your dream. Believing in something greater than yourself will enable you to trust in your dream. If you don't trust anything, you won't believe in anything. Trust relates to hope and without it, life becomes fearful and lonely. The number one person you should learn to trust is you. If you don't trust you, no-one will. You cannot trust anyone or anything without first trusting yourself. Trust gives us a sense of security and stability. It also gives us confidence to pursue the life of our dreams.

NOTES

CHAPTER THREE
Principle 5: Discover your purpose

While everyone wants to be successful, not everyone believes that success is attainable. A 2014 study conducted by Mission Australia found although nearly 90 percent of youths aged 15-19 had high career aspirations, only just over half believed they would be successful. This means too many young people are growing up not believing in their own potential during some of their most impressionable years. The study identified external factors such as economic uncertainty as reasons for low expectations. However TPS, though not mentioned, is also a factor when you consider the tendency to suppress our skills in order to fit in. In fact, Peeters acknowledged that TPS begins very early and may continue thereafter. He writes:

Among primary school children, those who know all the answers and show too much enthusiasm are at risk of being cut down and ostracised by their classmates — a practice which sometimes continues throughout the education system ... This does not mean that Australians, at any point in their lives, are not allowed to be ambitious; it does mean, however, that there is enormous pressure on them to downplay their achievements before they are being singled out.

This is particularly alarming when we consider how much importance young people place on gaining approval from their peers. A 2016 Mission Australia study found youths aged 15-19 valued friendship over everything else (i.e. family, physical and mental health and even financial security). This means they are more inclined to go above and beyond to keep their friends happy and maintain approval. Peeters does however point out a growing number of acceleration programs within schools that he attributes to growing "efforts to eradicate" bullying in general within schools. Ironically though, such programs are designed to create a safe space that honours high achievers yet does so by confining them and potentially isolating them.

Our gifts and our individuality should be honoured without confinement. There are over 7 billion people on this earth and with the exception of some twins, no two people have the same DNA. That means we all have our own unique genetic makeup. We are born different and destined to be unique. There is power in individuality. Every single person has unique skills and talents that no-one else can do quite like you. Some have discovered their talents, while others might still be discovering theirs. There is great value in honouring your uniqueness because it's what sets you apart from others. Whether it's a singing talent or having the gift of gab, everyone was born with something special to offer and now is the time to discover what yours is.

The achievements of tall poppies sometimes go ignored by those who are envious of them. So it is imperative that we as a society continue to evolve and learn to give credit where it's due. While some may think ignoring high achievers is harmless or unnecessary, experience proves otherwise. Recognition (i.e. awards, praise) is a great tool for encouraging high achievers in their success. It can also highlight skills and talents that a person otherwise may never have realised they event had.

In high school, english was my favourite subject. During year 11, my second last year before uni, I had a remarkable english teacher who I would never forget. One day in class, we had to write a creative story. He asked us to recall a memorable moment from our childhood and to write a story about it. I remembered a funny story and began jotting it down. I remember feeling passionate and excited as I brought my thoughts to life on paper. What's even better is the teacher loved the story.

"This piece is excellent. You are a natural writer Mibenge. You are going to go very far."

His simple words would remain in the back of my mind for years to come. It was at that moment that I realised I wanted to be a writer and it was all thanks to him. He pointed out a talent that I didn't even know existed. Up until that moment, my high school experience had been a complicated journey from insecurity to self-discovery. So my teacher's words meant a lot and led me to believe in myself. He didn't have to give me praise. He could have simply graded my paper and called it a day, but instead, he took the time to recognise my writing talent which in essence led me to realise it. Parents, guardians and teachers have the most important jobs in the world, because they have the power to influence, inspire and shape the lives of young people. By recognising tall poppies, we uplift humanity.

To discover your purpose, is to discover your power. But what exactly is power? According to the Merriam-Webster dictionary, power is *"the ability or right to control people or things."* However, true power comes from within. Knowing who you are, what you are here for and where you are going. True power is the ability to control your own destiny. Without true power, we become weak and helpless. Too many people subconsciously relinquish their power to others everyday. Negative thoughts are the quickest way to do this. Remember, *where energy flows intention goes*. If you spend even a minute out of each day envying someone else's life, you relinquish your power. This means you take time that could be used building your own success and instead, focus it on someone else. Negative thoughts lead to negative outcomes.

This is why it's important to channel your energy. Replace every negative thought with a positive. Doing this means you regain your power. It should be noted that ignoring negative thoughts is never a solution. In fact, the first thing you should do when you notice a negative thought is to acknowledge it. Hear it, process it but always make sure to release it. The way to release a negative thought is to find a solution to it. For example: negative thought - *I'm never going to be successful.* This thought should instantly be acknowledged as a lie because unless you can predict the future or unless you are committed to failure, you can't possibly know what the future holds. Instead, replace it with a positive thought: *I'm ready to change my situation so I'm going to find new ways to be successful.*

For some people, discovering your purpose is a straightforward process while for others it's not. However, it's essential that you are open-minded and honest with yourself so that you are better able to identify what motivates you and drives you. There is no set timeframe on how long this process takes. For some it could take minutes, for others it could take months or years. Your situation is unique so always be patient with yourself. Self-discovery is a beautiful process and when done correctly, you will always grow from it. Sometimes discovering your purpose might be as simple as making a list of everything that you are passionate about.

Or in some cases, drastic life situations or even tragedy will often lead to purpose. One of many inspiring people that I met in New York was a young man who spent years pursing his only passion of basketball. He played professionally for years and travelled around the world playing in different countries. He won numerous accolades and was considered to be a hero in his community. One day, a serious injury ended his once thriving career which understandably left him devastated.

He spent years believing that basketball was his life purpose so being told he could no longer play left him shattered and lost. Not long after this, his little sister, who was his only sibling, died unexpectedly. He felt unimaginable grief and at times, doubted his ability to go on. As with most cases of grief, time was his biggest healer. Though the pain of loss would never subside, he learned to live with it. As time went on, he discovered a new purpose — teaching. Although he could no longer play his favourite sport and live the lifestyle of a professional athlete, he found healing and fulfilment in sharing his knowledge with others. He said that while life would never be the same, he found some peace in helping others through teaching.

"Although I'll never feel complete after losing my only sister, I've found a new purpose in honouring her memory by serving others."

This man's story is proof that your purpose can change, but we will touch on that later in this book. Once you discover your purpose, it's time to pursue it. The number one reason that most people aren't living their best lives is fear. Fear of rejection, fear of what others will think, fear of failure. Feeding into fear has the power to paralyse you and cripple you, but only if you allow it to. One of the many beauties of life is that we have free will and the ability to make our own choices. You are never free from the consequence of your choices but you are absolutely free to make them. Time after time I have seen people, including myself, relinquish their power to fear. From fresh university graduates who are just starting out in their careers to successful entrepreneurs, with years of experience. No-one is immune from fear. Just like envy, fear is a natural emotion. It's simply your mind's way of protecting you from potential danger. We must be conscious of how respond to fear and learn to channel that energy into something positive. The next time you feel fear, take a moment to stop, observe and release.

Three steps to letting go of fear:

- Stop: Take a moment to acknowledge what it is you are feeling. Allow yourself to feel scared in that present moment. Know that what you are experiencing is natural and that you are feeling scared based on your life situation at the moment. Regardless of why you are fearful, accept that you feel that way based on your thoughts and experiences. The fear is in your mind.

- Observe: Understand why you are scared in that moment. Closely analyse the situation you are in. What specifically led you to feeling fearful? Are you in imminent danger? Is it a life or death situation? Is there any risk involved with allowing yourself to let go of fear and take your power back?

- Release: Accept that your desire for success and happiness is far greater than your fears. Feeling scared does not serve you and in fact, fear only blocks your journey to greatness. Where energy goes, intention flows. To live your best life, you cannot afford to waste energy on fear. Once you have identified the source of your fear, release it back into the universe. This can be done in any way that makes you comfortable. A great way to let anything go is to declare it gone mentally or out loud: I acknowledge this feeling, but it no longer serves me, so I am allowing myself to release it.

When I first moved to New York, I found myself fascinated with a reality show called The Real Housewives of New York. It is a show about half a dozen women, who live privileged and glamorous lifestyles. Upon first glance, it would appear shallow and vacuous but through closer observation their individual tales of success make for entertaining and potentially inspiring TV. As someone who grew up in a working-class family, I was always in awe of their fancy dinner parties and private jet lifestyles. With each episode I found myself growing more curious. At least half of them were successful entrepreneurs, with some coming from very humble beginnings.

Bethenny Frankel is the mastermind behind the Skinnygirl cocktail company, estimated to be worth over $100 million. Heather Thomson is the brains behind the lucrative Yummie fashion brand and Carole Radziwill has ties to the Kennedy family but is successful in her own right as a New York Times best-selling author. I had to meet them. One day I received a random invite to a fashion show in the Upper East Side through my work as a journalist. It was from one of the housewives. I enjoyed attending glamorous events. It was fun to mingle with New York socialites, celebrities, politicians and entrepreneurs. But I was always selective about what I attended. A famous New York DJ friend of mine once said: *"don't attend everything you are invited to, no matter how fabulous it may be because it's not a good look. Learn to be selective."*

This statement rang true because although the city of nearly nine million is the media capital of the world, the industry is small and after a while you begin to recognise the same media faces. One cold Tuesday evening, I attended the fashion show, where I would cover the red carpet. It was everything I expected, jam-packed with skinny models, heavily botoxed upper east side socialites, bored journalists and Bravo TV production staff. Attending these events always left a bad taste in my mouth but at the same time intrigued me. To my delight, I would get more than just the standard PR responses that I usually got from famous people on any given red carpet. The housewives would share with me how they were able to overcome fear and find their own individual success.

Carole is a New York Times best-selling author and former ABC journalist. She is also a widow — having lost her husband Anthony Radziwill, the cousin and best friend of John F. Kennedy Jr., years prior. She made her mark on RHONY as a down-to-earth and successful entrepreneur, who was often the voice of reason. Upon meeting her, she was polite and refreshingly humble. She spoke to me about letting go of fear to pursue her dreams.

"You can't listen to the haters out there that'll say, 'who do you think you are' but also in addition to that, you can't listen to your own head."

"If you have a passion for something you've just got to pursue it and it's going to be hard and you are gonna fall down a lot, but it'll be worth it in the end. And you just can't listen to your inner voice and also people around you — there are a lot of people who say they wish you well but they don't ... or just people who don't understand — who go 'well I don't understand how you can do that or why would you do that' ... you can't listen to any of that. It's really tunnel vision."

Her words resonated with me, particularly because so many people had questioned my decision to leave Melbourne and move to New York. Her words validated that there is power in letting go of fear and that if you don't believe in you, no one else will.

Carole's fellow costar and entrepreneur Heather, a married mother-of-two, shared her own take on letting go of fear to achieve success.

"I don't know if you find the courage to actually pursue your dreams, or you just throw caution to the wind and you go for it and you just take the risk."

"I think what happens in life too often times is that we listen to the second voice. The first voice says 'I want to' and the second voice says 'but how will you?' and you've got to calm the second voice and go with your gut. Don't be afraid to fail because you will fail and failure is not a failure, failure is a chance to learn ... a chance to educate yourself."

"You are that much stronger after you fall down and scrape your knee. So it's important that if you choose a path and you've invested a lot but you realise maybe the path isn't working, it's ok to let go and move forward. So listen to your first voice, not your second because the second will always be the voice of doubt. Go for it and don't be afraid. Giving up

has a really bad connotation, it doesn't mean giving up it means moving forward and moving on."

LuAnn de Lesseps, formerly known as countess from her first marriage to a wealthy French businessman, is a former model and mother-of-two who got married for a second time at the end of 2016. She went from being a nurse to living the life of her dreams as an international model. She spoke to me about the importance positive thinking.

"I say to women positive self talk. Always encourage yourself to say the right things to yourself, which is - I am great and if I don't think I'm great nobody else will. Take chances — you have to put yourself in the right place at the right time. You have to take chances in life and if it doesn't work out, you can always go home."

"I had an endless amount of curiosity ... I was always very curious so that kind of drove me and led me from one part of my life to another and things happen in life for a reason, so you are put in a place for a reason and you are meant to be there and then it's time for the next door to be open."

Ramona Singer, a divorced mother-of-one who is the epitome of a New York socialite, said the law of attraction often helps her overcome fear.

"You just have to dig down deep and have the confidence and the will power, think four steps ahead and only think

positive thoughts. You know I think positive energy creates positive results, negative energy creates negative. The glass is half full, not half empty."

Manhattan mother-of-two, Kristen Taekman, a fashion Model and wife of successful supplement entrepreneur Josh Taekman , said letting go of fear is never easy but essential to achieve anything in life.

"I think you just have to keep that drive, just every day chip away at it little by little and don't take no for an answer. My husband [Josh] is really really good at that, he's really good motivation wise."

"It's just one door closes and another one opens, you just have to keep at it. And if it was easy everybody would do it. I say that so many times: 'oh my Gosh this is really hard' and it's like 'well Kristen if it was easy everybody would do it.'"

Over the years I would meet countless successful people, some famous, some not. Their message was always the same — don't give in to fear. To discover your purpose, remove all barriers that are standing in your way. Negative thoughts and feelings act as barriers between where we are and where we want to be. Sometimes we may not even be conscious of our own negativity. Whether it stems from incidents from our past, or worries about the future, holding on to bitterness or fear will only block you from success.

Take action:

Apologise. Forgive. Liberate.

It's time to release all negative energy. You should first accept all that you cannot change and let go of your past. It's time to forgive and move forward. This means forgiving anyone and everyone who has hurt you and who has done wrong by you. Forgiveness is the only way to set yourself free from pain, so that you can finally move forward with your life. It's time to take back your power and the first step in achieving this, is to first forgive yourself.

This is often the most difficult part. Forgive yourself for not always honouring yourself, for selling yourself short and for not knowing your true self-worth. Also forgive yourself for all the pain you knowingly and unknowingly caused other. Without first learning how to forgive yourself, you cannot forgive others. People are always quick to point out how they have been hurt and let down by others but they are not as quick to remember all of those times that they hurt or disappointed others.

Now that you have completed the internal and external cleanse, it is important to make peace with your past to start your new beginning. On a piece of paper, write down a list of times that you have mistreated others. There is no minimum or maximum number, just take note of all of the key moments that you can recall. Try to determine why it is that you acted the way that you did in a bid to understand your behaviour in those moments. Try to remember how your actions made the other person feel. Then apologise (either mentally or out loud) for the role you played in causing their hurt. Once you have done this, forgive yourself for choosing fear in that moment and allowing your insecurities to get the better of you. Make a promise to yourself to choose love over fear going forward and then finally, release those negative memories.

Too many people will go through their entire lives holding on to bitterness and resentment. Doing this only hinders your personal growth and obstructs your path to greatness. It is perfectly ok to acknowledge painful ordeals that you have endured and it is also ok to be hurt and upset, but you cannot afford to hold onto your emotions because eventually they will consume you. For example, feeling bitter and angry at someone who mistreated you is natural. But holding on to those feelings is unhealthy. Let go and give yourself permission to move on.

Throughout life, people will mistreat you and disrespect you but it's up to you as to whether you dwell in it or rise above it. You can either relinquish your power by feeding into your emotions or you can forgive them, let it go and move forward. Never take on someone else's internal struggle by responding to a negative situation with a negative reaction.

One of the hardest challenges in life is to forgive without ever having received an apology. Forgiveness is one of the most powerful tools there is to help you make peace with your past.

The late Nelson Mandela, who was falsely imprisoned for 27 years and who is one of the world's greatest heroes, once famously said: *"As I walked out the door toward the gate that would lead to my freedom, I knew if I didn't leave my bitterness and hatred behind, I'd still be in prison."*

Despite enduring years of torture and unjust punishment, he refused to stay bitter and angry. Instead of relinquishing his power to those who wronged him, he made a conscious decision to forgive them. Even though he could never get back the nearly three decades of his life that were essentially stolen from him, he chose to forgive. He knew that if he didn't, he could never truly move forward and go on to live his best life.

Make a list of all the key moments that you have been mistreated in your life. Again, there is no minimum or maximum moments, just as many as you still hold on to today. Once you have completed your list, fold the paper in half twice and then place it between both hands and close your eyes. The next step is to meditate and be still, or do whatever it is you do to connect with the universe. Repeat the following, either mentally or out loud: "I forgive all of those who have hurt or mistreated me. I am releasing this memory so that I can move forward in peace.

RECAP

Apologise: Learn to say sorry and apologise quickly. Many people fail to realise that there is actually great strength and power in being able to admit your wrongs and accept responsibility. We all make mistakes because none of us are perfect and the sooner we can accept this, the better off we are. Once you acknowledge your mistakes, you give yourself permission to let go and move on. It is important that you take note of all of your past mistakes so that you can avoid repeating them. Apologise for your own bad behaviour and then forgive yourself and promise to act differently in the future.

Forgive: Once you forgive yourself, you can then forgive others. Release all of the pain and hurt that you have bottled up inside so that you can finally break free from the chains of your past. In chapters one and two you eliminated all sources of pain and hurt from your life and now it's time to let go of all of the lingering sources of toxicity which includes painful memories that you might have buried deep within your psyche. Some people tend to assume that the only way you can forgive someone is if they beg for forgiveness through an apology but the reality is that you will not always receive the apology you deserve. In fact, many times that others hurt you, they may not always acknowledge their wrong doing and thus you are left with deep emotional scars that are in need of healing. Once you learn to forgive others without receiving an apology, you allow yourself to move on and heal thus reclaiming the very power they tried to take from you.

Liberate: Free yourself from your painful past to make room for your bright future. Holding on to anger and resentment only hinders your ability to grow and prevents you from living the life of your dreams. The energy that you invest in honouring fear and frustration only takes away from the work that is required to achieve your goals. Stop worrying and start doing. It is time to shift your thinking and acknowledge the beauty in the pain you have endured. What doesn't kill you makes you stronger. Learn to channel your frustrations into passion in a bid to birth your dreams.

NOTES

CHAPTER FOUR
Principle 4: Take back your power

Ever notice how tall poppies are never sitting around envying others? They don't spend their days on the phone with their friends gossiping or speaking negatively about others. Instead, they're usually focused on expanding their success. The reason for this is simple - Where energy goes, intention flows. Successful people understand that time is valuable. They cannot afford to spend their time bringing others down. It serves as no use and is destructive. Now that you have discovered your purpose, it's time to make it a reality.

In order to take back your power, you will need to have focus. Anytime you think a negative thought, you lose focus and relinquish some of your power. Staying focused is something that most tall poppies struggle with at some point.

Successful entrepreneurs are constantly flooded with great business ideas, but in most cases, they will direct most of their focus on one to avoid spreading themselves too thin. Without focus, you lose direction. Without direction, you lose sight of your purpose. If you are not clear about your purpose, you cannot succeed. We've all heard someone talk about having a cool business idea one day then weeks later, it disappears and it's never spoken about again. Or someone who has dreams of making it in Hollywood and months later, they're still in their 9-5 office job making excuses for not pursuing their dreams. These people lack focus. They may have tapped into their purpose but without focus, lost sight of their own dreams. Learn to take your dreams seriously. This starts with first taking yourself seriously.

Australians are widely adored around the world for their humility and self-deprecating humour. Anytime you hear a foreigner talking about an Aussie, you will often hear the terms "down to earth", "easy going" and "chilled out" in describing our culture and personalities. These are all great qualities to have and one of many reasons that Aussies are so well-liked. However, there is a common misconception among ourselves that recognising or celebrating your own success is not in line with Aussie values and therefore somehow "unAustralian." This is a lie. Humility and success are not mutually exclusive. What you will often hear from those who suffer from TPS is *"he's getting to big for his boots"* or *"she needs to come back down to reality."* For these people, the word success holds a negative connotation as it is often associated with arrogance and egotism. This mentality is flawed and it relates back to fear and envy.

If you do not take yourself serious, no one else will. Naturally, when it comes to your purpose, there should be an overwhelming sense of passion and excitement that surrounds it. If there isn't, you have yet to discover your true purpose. The way you feel about your purpose will determine how others receive it. Be bold and unafraid when it comes to pursuing your dreams and understand that failure is not the end. Take back your power by overcoming fear. Too many of us don't believe entirely believe in our dream to start with and wonder why we don't succeed. Once you have discovered your purpose, it is essential that you retrain your mind to wholeheartedly trust and believe that you are on the right path in pursing it.

To take back your power is to earn respect. When you talk, people should listen. Have you ever been to a seminar or lecture where the audience struggled to pay attention to the speaker? Chances are, the speaker was bored and unexcited about whatever it is they were presenting and that energy spilled out into the crowd. If you are not passionate, no one else will be. If you don't believe in your product, you are wasting your time. When I lived in New York, I had the privilege of watching some of the greatest speakers in the world. I noticed they always left their crowd feeling motivated and inspired. Some people literally sat at the edge of their seat throughout the talk. Each speaker instantly captivated their audience from the moment they hit the stage and they always left them wanting more. These speakers all had one thing in common — they spoke with passion and authenticity which showed they truly believed in what they spoke about.

It's ok to not feel passionate about your purpose, that simply means you haven't actually discovered your true purpose. The biggest mistake that some people make is to try and hide their lack of passion. Whether it's because they've invested a lot and don't want to risk losing everything, or they're simply too proud to try something new — they refuse to give up. We've all encountered desperate salespeople or aggressive marketers. While they may be persistent, their lack of passion about what it is they're selling is prevalent and completely turns you off. When you are honest with yourself and your intentions are pure, passion comes naturally. It's time to take your power back.

The universe always responds to our thoughts and actions. When you are open to life and your intentions are good, you are rewarded. Maybe not instantly, but in due course. Start speaking life into your dreams. The power of words goes far beyond conversation. Language affects the thought process and tells the mind what to believe, while also manifesting thoughts into the universe. It is imperative that you choose your words wisely. Taking back your power requires confidence. Shift from saying *"I can't"* and *"I don't"* to *"I can"* and *"I will."* Positive affirmations are essential on your journey to success.

Sometimes you may not mean what you say or say what you mean, but your words (subconscious or otherwise) have a huge impact. We live in a society that is constantly coining new words and phrases. One particular phrase that has grown popular in recent years is *"I can't,"* or alternatively *"I can't deal…"* and *"I can't even."* The phrase is American and used to convey someone's inability to understand an outrageous situation or person. It is often used in a mocking sense, sometimes in conjunction with other urban phrases like *"bye Felicia"* or *"girl bye."* Regardless of context, saying *"I can't"* means *"I'm unable."* This is a negative affirmation that manifests self-doubt. Be conscious of the language you use. Choosing positive words sends positive affirmations to your mind and to the universe, which ultimately promotes success.

By planning my move to New York to pursue my dreams, I was subconsciously sending a message to the universe that I was ready to live my best life. I could have taken the easy route and did what most people do, which is dream big and never act on it. Many people often visualise their dreams but fail to implement any effective strategies. They instead find comfort in mediocrity and make excuses. *How will I support myself if I quit my job? I'm married with kids, it's too late for me. It will never work, I'm gonna fail why bother?* These excuses are just ways to justify not having enough courage to live your best life.

Just because you want to model in Europe, doesn't mean you have to quit your retail job in Sydney and move to Paris right away. All change should be planned well in advance and it should be gradual. Patience is a virtue and you will need lots of it. Big dreams take time, they rarely ever happen over night so it's important that you accept this. Impatience will kill your dreams. Time and time again, I've watched others quit prematurely because they wanted instant results and lacked patience. This often occurs in the race against time. When we feel as though it's "too late" to achieve our dreams, it's easy to become impatient. The key is to understand that success does not discriminate.

A friend of mine was convinced that it was "too late" for him to pursue his dreams because he was in his 30s. Up until that point, he had lived a relatively simple life in Melbourne but always knew in the back of his mind that he had far more to offer. One day, he found the courage to pursue his dreams of working in investment banking. Within months, he was admitted to an Ivy league school in the US and he is now a top investment banker on Wall Street. He credited self-belief, which was instilled by his mother at a young age, for his ability to pursue success.

"My mum always told me I was destined for greatness, so I never ever forgot the measure of myself. As I got older, a part of me thought I might have missed my boat but I remembered life has no timeline. Success doesn't follow a set calendar. Whenever I doubted myself, I'd ask which option would make a better story. And this is what led me to where I am today, and will guide me to where I want to be in the near future."

Most successful entrepreneurs can attest to the fact that their dreams did not come to life overnight. What can happen overnight though, is making the necessary changes in life in preparation for future success. If you are an aspiring actor why not sign up for acting classes? If you've always dreamed of becoming a nurse, perhaps now is the time to finally enrol in nursing school. Just as you would with a savings account, you need to invest in your future by making regular manifestation deposits. Take the necessary steps towards making your dreams a reality. Dreaming up an idea and hoping for the best is simply not enough. Do your part by putting in the work to initiate change. No more excuses, no more doubts. The time is now and the change starts with you.

It's vital that you believe in your own power to achieve any success. There is a common misconception that power is tangible but this is a lie. True power is in your mind. It's an energy that you develop naturally once you have mastered the art of believing in yourself. Many people do not consider themselves to be powerful because they focus on lack and the things they don't have. *I don't drive a fancy car or my home is not fancy enough.* Focusing on lack will only hinder your growth. Learn to appreciate everything you *do* have. This does not mean material goods. In fact, focusing on "stuff" will almost always leave you feeling empty and unfulfilled.

Purpose should not be confused with money. While it is true that doing what you love often leads to financial abundance, making money should never be mistaken as the purpose itself. I once met a self-made millionaire who told me that despite having achieved his dream of having millions of dollars in the bank, he was miserable. Born and raised in Mississippi, he spent years running successful nightclubs around the US and while he had made a lot of money, he felt lonely and unfulfilled. He couldn't understand the overwhelming feeling of emptiness because he had convinced himself that making money was his purpose, but it wasn't. He eventually realised that getting involved in his local church brought him great joy. He started a ministry and before long, he forged a new career helping others through faith. He said that while making money was never his purpose, he was grateful because it gave him the means to devote all of his time to church — which makes him happy.

"Everyone assumes money equals happiness and I can tell you that simply isn't true. It buys freedom to an extent but I was miserable when I was focused on staying rich. I do however thank God for the experience because it led me to my happiness, my purpose."

Too many people focus on superficial aspects of life. As a society, although we have become more conscious as a whole, we are more shallow than ever. Everyone wants the latest smartphone or the best clothes. Many people wake up miserable each day because they believe they don't have enough. We are a society consumed by greed and impatience. We want more "stuff" quickly and technology facilitates our excessive consumption. For example, we've all seen someone who has ruined their appearance with plastic surgery. They probably looked fine pre-surgery but eventually gave in to insecurity by going under the knife. And months later got something else done. Then months after that went back because they *still* weren't satisfied. This is because they're pursuing a shallow and empty dream.

There is no power in material or superficial goods. The sooner you accept that true power comes from within, the sooner you can finally begin your journey to happiness. True power is mental and it comes from self-worth and self-acceptance. When you know who you are and why you are here (your life purpose), you begin to live with intent. Your outlook on life is clearer and you gain more self-confidence.

Stop focusing on material goods and learn to value substance.

Take action

Focus. Command. Grow.

To take back your power is to take control. It's time to stop letting other people control your life. You are the master of your own destiny. Relying on others for praise wand waiting around for someone to hopefully one day notice how great you are without taking any initiative, will get you nowhere. Learn to trust yourself and your ideas, to develop inner confidence. If you don't believe in your own potential, you won't believe in or support others. It is also important that you do no self-sabotage. Sometimes, even after establishing our purpose, we will doubt or question it. Do you speak positively about your dreams? Do you recopies your own talents and achievements?

Some people will subconsciously speak negatively about my dreams, which manifests failure. You should avoid comments like: *"hopefully it all works out"* and *"if it's not successful then... ."* While it is pivotal that you are realistic and honest with yourself, your focus should never be on negative affirmations. Instead, focus on what is working or what success will look like.

Three key points to remember:

- Focus: Always remember what is important. Your purpose should be at the forefront of every decision that you make. If it doesn't elevate you or help you achieve success, let it go. Be conscious of your space. Anything or anyone that's ever been great in life has more than likely required intense focus. This means obsessively thinking about your goals and constantly finding new ways to achieve them. You cannot afford to worry about others. What people think or what they're doing should never be your concern. Remember, comparison is the thief of joy. If you have time to sit around envying others, you are not serious about your life. Successful people do not invest time in others, they invest time in themselves.

- Command: You must take charge of your life to be taken seriously. Your life is in your hands and it should always stay that way. The minute we hand over the keys to someone else, we lose our independence and our purpose. No other human being will make you successful in life. It's up to you to take control and make things happen. You determine what kind of life you want and how you are going to achieve it. You should always exude passion and excitement about your purpose. The words you speak and the actions you take have a direct impact on how successful you will be. Learn to take yourself seriously. Always be conscious of the energy you bring into a room. Energy is contagious. If you are desperate, or disinterested or unhappy, those feelings will manifest.

- Grow: Just as plants need water to survive, our dreams need positive affirmations. A dream without action is pure fantasy. Make it your duty to discover your purpose and plan logical ways to achieve it. Your path to greatness requires new and innovative ways of thinking. Old ways of thinking will produce more of the same. Trust in your journey and be open to failure. Be honest with yourself and if something isn't working, always be sure to learn from your mistakes. There will be ups and downs so it is important that you never lose hope. Your persistence will pay off.

RECAP

Desire: Picture what success looks like. If you could live the life of your dreams tomorrow, what would that entail? Would you be a famous actress? A doctor? A Mother? All of the above? Whatever your answer is, know that it is possible. Give yourself permission to live your best life. Stop making excuses and start honouring your talents. Life is not a rehearsal, you only get one shot. Most people don't bother to chase their desires because they don't believe they are worthy of living their best life. At this point, you should have a renewed sense of self. You should be feeling uplifted and inspired. You should wholeheartedly believe that anything is possible.

Encourage: You should be your own biggest cheerleader. Give yourself permission to be successful by reminding yourself that you are worthy of happiness. Remember, there is great value in your uniqueness and individuality. Whatever makes you different should be embraced and celebrated. Focus on manifesting positive affirmations buy remembering what is possible, rather than what is not. Thoughts and words have the power to make or break dreams, you should therefore be conscious of your thought patterns. The universe responds to your thoughts and words accordingly, so always speak life into your dreams. How you feel about something will almost always reflect on the outside.

Implement: Once you have envisioned what you want, it's time to create your action plan. How do you intend to get to where it is you are going? It is highly encouraged that you take some time to do this properly. Consider how long it will take and what resources are required. Many people will often be discouraged at this stage because planning can be overwhelming. Do not lose hope. If you do not have the resources (i.e. money, time) at that moment, wait until your do. There are no excuses for giving up. Stay focused, water the seeds you plant and take charge. Practice patience as you develop your plan and ensure that you see it through.

People will often dream about who it is they want to become, yet act nothing like that person. No matter how many great ideas, plans or dreams you have, if you are not actively trying to become the person it is you want to be — you are wasting your time. A wise person once said: fake it 'til you make it. This means you need to walk the talk. There's no use dreaming about one day opening up your own environmentalist organisation if you don't even recycle. Or telling everyone how you want to become a fashion model but eating junk food everyday. No one will take you seriously and you probably need to rethink your purpose.

Too many people talk about what they're going to do once they "make it" but this thinking is wrong. You need to start becoming who it is you want to be right away. The way you speak, they way you dress, the way you live should be in line with who you want to be. The notion that you'll someone become more environmentally conscious once you've got the money to open your environmentalist organisation is unrealistic. If you work in an entry level job and your dream is to one day run your own company, you should think and act like a CEO. Consider doing part-time study, or attending leadership seminars. Anything that will bring you closer to achieving your dreams will benefit you. If your dream is to one day become a politician, get to know your community and start keeping up with political news. As soon as you initiate change, you take control of your destiny.

NOTES

CHAPTER FIVE

Principle 3: Trust yourself

Trust takes years to build and seconds to lose. Sometimes when it's lost, it can never be regained. Without trust, there is no relationship. This applies to the relationship you have with yourself and with others. Trust is essential. You often hear divorced people saying their marriage simply couldn't be repaired because "the trust was gone," or people ending years-long friendships over trust-related issues. One of the greatest challenges that we face in life is the ability to trust ourselves. The Mirriam-Webster dictionary defines the word *trust* as *"belief that someone or something is reliable, good, honest, effective, etc."*

Your ability to trust others will depend on your ability to trust yourself. The reason that people struggle to trust themselves usually stems from past experience. It goes back to the conditioning and what we're taught (Chapter Two). From a young age, we're taught to seek outward approval for our own validation. From our parents to our teachers, we relied on others to let us know whether we were trustworthy. Think back to when you first got your pen license or the first time you were left you in charge of the classroom. These moments likely made you feel validated and good. You probably felt more reassured in who you are and confident in trusting yourself.

Now remember a time when were made to feel the opposite. Perhaps you were the last to be picked by your peers during a class activity or maybe you were overlooked for an award that you felt you deserved. This no doubt made you feel rejected and sad. You likely began to doubt yourself and started believing that you are untrustworthy. While some people might brush this off as common childhood occurrences, it should be noted that this habit of relying on others for validation often continues into adulthood. From your work to your love life, unless you have learned how to wholeheartedly trust yourself, chances are you still rely on others for validation.

Think about a time that your job application was rejected or when your significant other said they didn't trust you. You would've felt terrible and in some cases maybe believed you weren't good enough. This pattern of behaviour is destructive and has to go. You will never truly trust yourself if you continue relying on others for approval. What they think about you is none of your business. What you think about you is what matters. You will never completely trust another person until you trust yourself. It begins with you and the qualities that make up your character. There are many elements of trust, including honesty, reliability and loyalty.

How honest, reliable and loyal you are to yourself determines how much you can trust yourself and others. In order to be honest with yourself, take time to get to know who you are. This means honouring your values, staying true to yourself and being consistent. Dishonesty shows a lack of dignity and self-confidence. Reliability requires you to be dependable and stable — meaning that you are available and present no matter what. Unreliability creates uncertainty and insecurity. To be loyal means to be completely devoted and committed. When you are disloyal, you lack transparency. Trusting yourself can be a complex and life-long process for some while for others, it comes naturally. Every decision that you make in life will indicate whether or not you trust yourself. Your career, your relationships, your thought patterns — everything is influenced by trust. There are three key ingredients that can help you learn to trust yourself.

- Self-awareness: Knowing your identity and your value in the world helps cultivate trust. When you know who you are, you know what you want. Having confidence in yourself and your environment promotes self-awareness. This means being sure of your decisions. The type of job you want, the type of mate you want, even the kind of house you want to live in. You take ownership of your life and work to achieve your goals. We've all met confident people. Those people who walk into a room and radiate powerful energy. The ones who never second-guess themselves. The ones who speak with conviction. The only difference between them and you is that they've learned how to accept and trust themselves.

- Self-respect: Your goal should be to develop true self-confidence. This comes by learning how to trust yourself. However, another vital ingredient is self-respect. Have you ever met someone who appears to ooze confidence? They're usually loud, intense or perhaps even slightly obnoxious. They come across as having high self-esteem and enjoy attention — they might even seek it at times. However, when it comes to certain aspects in their life (i.e. love and relationships) they completely lack self-respect. This is because their projected self-confidence is a facade. True confidence cannot be attained without self-respect. They generally go hand-in-hand. It should be noted that confidence is more than just a feeling, but also a way of life. When you learn to fully accept and love yourself, you naturally feel confident and self-respect for who you are. Respecting yourself means putting yourself first, honouring your happiness and giving yourself permission to live your best life.

- Integrity: Having values, morals and principles to live by gives us a foundation and structure in our lives. We begin forming our values from a very young age. This means, what we believe in, what we honour, who we respect and how we live our lives. For some people, integrity is closely tied to their faith in that religion dictates their values, morals and principles. For others, it is learned behaviour in that they adopted the same values, morals and principles as their parents. To achieve true integrity is to honour your values. While every person's values will differ, there are fundamental elements that should form the basis of those values:

- Ethics
- Transparency
- Respect
- Conscientiousness

Before you can truly begin to trust yourself, you must really get to know yourself. Dating is a fascinating and fun way to get to know someone. It can also be a great way to discover your true self. While it may sound like an odd concept, dating yourself builds self-confidence which helps cultivate self-love. Without these qualities, you won't like the person you are and therefore will not trust yourself. *As the saying goes, if you don't love you no one else will.*

Many of us want to learn self-love but we simply don't know how. Dating yourself enables you to get to know yourself on a deeper level and eventually fall in love with yourself. As you would do any given dating situation, it's important that you spend time getting to know your likes and dislikes, your joys and woes, your interests and your disinterests. What makes you happy? What makes you sad? What food do you most like? What kind of music do you enjoy? While these may seem like basic questions, they are significant because they hold the key to unlocking your true self.

People who suffer from TPS are an example of how a lack of self-love can be harmful and self-destructive. When you don't love yourself, it is difficult to love other people. Ever noticed how unhappy people are constantly pointing out other people's flaws and failures? These people never recognise the success of others and they cut others down at any given opportunity. But tall poppies encourage the success of others. People who have achieved self-love prefer to support and praise others rather than criticise and judge them. These people tend to live happier and more fulfilled lives.

There are many ways in which you can achieve self-love. Below is a list of ideas for dating yourself:

- Solo date: Go to the movies, take yourself out to dinner, visit a museum or go for a walk in beautiful park. Set a date, time and place and commit to it. The goal is to pick something that you genuinely enjoy doing and make time for yourself to enjoy it. If you are not comfortable being around you, how can you expect anyone else to?

- Travel alone: Pick a destination. Pack a bag and jump on a plane/train/bus etc, whether it's for one night or one year. Traveling alone somewhere foreign is an eye-opening and exciting way to challenge yourself mentally and emotionally while also learning about yourself.

- Pamper yourself: A day at the spa can be therapeutic and remedial. When your body is relaxed, your mind is relaxed. Always acknowledge hard work and take time to reward yourself. Making time for yourself shows self-worth and self-appreciation.

- Spring clean: Out with the old, in with the new. Reorganising and rearranging your sacred space invites new energy and creates a more healthy living environment. Set a day and time aside to declutter and clean out everything from your home to your cell phone. Cleaning eliminates negative energy and attracts higher vibrations.

- Positive affirmations: Take time out of your day to sit somewhere quiet and write a list of all the things that make you great. This can be done wherever you feel comfortable. Take a couple of minutes to gather your thoughts before you write. Complete the following sentence by inserting an adjective into the blank space and filling out the rest. Do this using every adjective listed below. When the list is complete, place it somewhere around the house that is easily visible for you see it daily (e.g.: bedroom wall, bathroom mirror, fridge etc)

  I am ____ because....

  Adjectives: appreciated, kind, happy, important, loved, successful, valued.

Take action:

Embrace. Monitor. Affirm.

At this stage, you should feel more confident about your purpose and more open to trusting yourself. It is important that you are patient as you complete this process. Change will not be instant but the overall results will be life-changing. Always remain focused and committed to achieving your goals. It will be challenging and at times overwhelming but never give up. You picked up this his book because deep down, you know that you deserve to live your best life. You know that you are worthy, capable and destined for greatness. It is up to you to trust this message and do the necessary work to succeed.

Once you learn to trust yourself, you can trust others and learn to believe in your purpose. Without a sense of belief, we risk losing direction, the future appears murky and we become stagnant and unmotivated. Growing up, I was always encouraged by my parents to love myself and believe in my dreams — but this was not always easy to do. When I first told family and friends about my dreams of moving to NYC, I received little support. They couldn't understand why I would give up a life of security and stability to pursue the unknown. The negative responses were not shocking, rather disappointing. I still vividly recall feeling excited about my plans to pursue my dreams but I was constantly met with criticism and skepticism. While in hindsight I realise the negative reactions stemmed from a lack of understanding, at the time it was discouraging. It became so disheartening that at one point, I began to doubt myself.

This is another example of why it's important to monitor your surroundings. Others doubted me and I started to believe them. In Chapter One, we looked at the importance of eliminating toxic energy and being conscious of your social circle. TPS is not only destructive but also contagious. Fortunately, I realised this early on and eventually I removed myself from the situation before it could really affect me. I learned to trust myself years prior and was therefore able to block out the negativity. There is only one voice that truly matters and that is your own. When you learn to pay attention to your inner voice (or intuition as some call it), you begin to trust yourself. Train your mind to think positively. When you shift your thinking, your inner voice gains clarity and positive thinking becomes a habit. Trusting and believing in yourself is a choice and it all starts from within.

The most common element that blocks our ability to trust is fear. Too often we waste time worrying about the unknown and things that we cannot control or change. At times that we should be open to trust, we often become plagued with fear. We begin to ask questions like "what if things don't work out," "What if I fail?" or "what will others think?"

Too often, we allow the fear of failure to outweigh the possibility of success. The trick to breaking this cycle is learning how to choose trust over fear. The key to success in any area of life requires a certain level of trust so you should allow the possibility of success to be greater than any fears or doubts. You will never fully be able to trust while finding contentment in fear. So your focus should be entirely on succeeding rather than failing. It is important to note that being trustful does not somehow make you immune from failure, it simply means that you no longer fear it.

Failure should not be feared for several reasons, most importantly because it is never final. What counts is your response to failure. Some of the most accomplished people in the world became successful by refusing to give up. They were undeterred, relentless and motivated even after repeatedly failing. *What is meant for you will not surpass you.* We are all destined for greatness, it's simply up to us to achieve it.

Trust is a form of gratitude. By expressing gratitude in our lives we acknowledge our own achievements and manifest success. There are many ways that you can express gratitude. Some people pray, others meditate, others give back to charity. There is no right of wrong way, each person should do what their comfortable with. The most important thing is that you do in fact practice gratitude on a regular basis. Below are some examples of how you can manifest more success into your life.

Practice Gratitude

- Pray: Each morning when you wake up, say a prayer before you start your day. Regardless of your beliefs, this is a great way to connect with your higher self or source. Acknowledge the good and bad in your situation. Taking a moment to give thanks for even the smallest blessing promotes peace, love and trust.

- Meditate: By taking just a few minutes out of the day for yourself, you take a step towards achieving greater self-love. Meditation means different things to different people. Traditionally, it involves sitting in silence to connect with source. This has been scientifically proven to promote peace and relaxation.

- Charity: Giving back is a selfless gesture. Whether it's donating to a clothing bin or feeding the homeless, charity goes a very long way because in helping others you are also helping yourself mentally and spiritually. Giving to others makes us feel valued and gives us a sense of purpose.

- Spread positive energy: We all have a moral obligation to leave the world in better condition than we found it in. In a world that is filled with war, terror and suffering, we must make a conscious effort to spread hope, happiness and love. Be conscious of the way in which you treat others. Smile at strangers, open doors, say *"thank you"* and compliment others. Good energy makes for a great environment.

RECAP

Learn: Take the time to discover who you are and what interests you. Everything from the types of foods you enjoy to the kind of friends you want should be carefully considered. While many people assume that they already know everything that there is to know about themselves, this is often not the case. When you have established true self-worth and when you are truly connected to your true self, nothing and none can break that bond that you have with yourself. No man or woman can come in and take control of your life or change who you are. It is important that you invest time in getting to know yourself on a deep level. The best way to get to know yourself is to date yourself. Be sure to invest in alone time, particularly outdoors. Discovering what makes you happy builds understanding and boosts self-esteem, thus giving you a greater sense of life purpose.

Accept: Once you discover your true self, you can work towards building self acceptance. If you cannot accept yourself as you are, you will never be able to accept others. Be kind to yourself and ensure that your thoughts remain positive. Speak highly of yourself and your dreams and fill your mind with positive affirmations. Eliminate negative thinking and avoid saying *"I can't"* or *"I'm not."* Instead, replace these terms with more positive sayings like *"I can"* and *"I will."*

Be: Be comfortable in your own skin and learn to be yourself. Instead of pointing out and dwelling over every flaw and imperfection, learn to celebrate all of the unique things that make you — YOU. When your Mind, Body and Spirit is in synch you will be centred and at peace with yourself. When this occurs, you are in the best possible position for change. Learn to calm your thoughts and trust in yourself. Understand that change is necessary and believe that it is in your best interest.

Failure is inevitable but it's important that you don't get discouraged by this. There is no person on earth who has had any type of success without first having experienced failure. In fact, most successful people that I've met have always been motivated by their failure — which eventually led them to victory. When you finally have the courage to pursue your purpose, you will constantly be met with rejection, resistance and other setbacks. The key is to never be deterred by this. Learn to view rejection as a tool pushing you closer to success. Always see the silver lining in every situation. Every *"no"* is a step towards you finally hearing a *"yes."*

Trust your gut every time, it will never fail you. In order for you to make the best decisions, you need the support of people who believe in you and who encourage your ideas. Constructive feedback is great but you cannot afford to have naysayers and negative people around you. In Chapter One, you eliminated all sources of toxicity and it is vital that you maintain clean space. It is ok to be selective about who you embrace because it's up to you to protect your dream. Doing this shows self-love and self-worth.

NOTES

CHAPTER SIX
Principle 2: Live with intention

Most of us live on autopilot. We've become a nation of zombies who rely on others to take control of our lives, as we travel along in a comatose state to an unknown destination. We go to work and do just enough to get by and pay the bills, come home, eat, sleep and repeat. If you are fortunate enough, you'll get a two-day weekend — which for some ends up being a drunken blur to forget about life even just for a moment.

We're constantly pressed for time and rarely ever present. No matter how desperate we are for change, we tell ourselves we're "too busy" to improve our situation and simply throw it on the back burner. One of my favourite movies of all time is Simon West's 90s blockbuster Con Air.

In one scene, serial killer Garland Greene (played by Steve Buscemi), shares his take on what it means to be "insane."

"What if I told you insane was working 50 hours a week in some office for fifty years, at the end of which they tell you to piss off. Ending up in some retirement village, hoping to die before suffering the indignity of trying to make it to the toilet on time. Wouldn't you consider that to be insane?"

The last thing anyone wants is to feel overwhelming regret while lying on their deathbed but this is a common reality for many people. Australian nurse Bronnie Ware wrote about this in her 2012 book *The Top Five Regrets of the Dying*. In it, she identified the number one regret that people have before death after having spent years with sick patients in their final moments. The most common regret was not having pursued their dreams. She wrote:

1. *I wish I'd had the courage to live a life true to myself, not the life others expected of me.*

   This was the most common regret of all. When people realise that their life is almost over and look back clearly on it, it is easy to see how many dreams have gone unfulfilled. Most people had not honoured even a half of their dreams and had to die knowing that it was due to choices they had made, or not made. It is very important to try and honour at least some of your

> *dreams along the way. From the moment that you lose your health, it is too late. Health brings a freedom very few realise, until they no longer have it.*

Taking the first step in pursuing your dreams is always the hardest. But what is no doubt even harder is living with regret. No one was destined to work 40-plus hours a week in a job they hate and die, and no one is destined to be miserable. Every single human being on this planet has something incredible to offer the world. It's simply up to us to discover what that incredible gift is. The problem is that most people do not live with intention. Tall poppies have mastered the art of this, but for others, this is likely something they've never even heard of.

So what exactly is living with intention? The Mirriam-Webster dictionary defines the word "intend" as "to have in mind as a purpose or goal." Therefore to have intention is to have purpose. In Chapter Three, you learned that your purpose is your power. Living with intention means using your power. So many of us simply go with the flow in life instead of taking charge. We sit back and relax as life unfolds before our cry eyes. However, to live your best life, you have to be willing to break out of the comforts of ordinary life. No more watching tall poppies from the sidelines, it's your time to shine.

There are four P's needed to live with intention:

- Purpose
- Pride
- Project
- Plan

Purpose: We previously went over how to discover your purpose and here we will explore adapting to change as it relates to your purpose. Life changes by the second. People, circumstances, technology even the weather — we experience change on a regular basis. The same applies to your purpose. Discovering your purpose is a great feeling but what happens when your purpose changes? Many people don't realise that you can have more than one purpose in life. In fact, this applies to most people.

A change in purpose should not scare you, but instead excite you. After all, new beginnings mean new opportunities. Where we begin to hit stumbling blocks is when we fail to identify a change in purpose. Often, we will mistake this for failure or lack of passion. The power lies in knowing when it's time to move on. Many people will go against the grain instead of adapting to change. The universe will always drop hints to validate that you are on the right path, it's important to pay close attention. If you are no longer passionate about the successful business you built 10 years ago, it might be time to either change your role within the business or sell it so that you can start pursuing your new purpose. Change is inevitable and the sooner we adapt, the sooner we can begin living fulfilled lives.

Pride: The number one thing that drives tall poppies is their passion and with passion comes motivation. You will never accomplish what it is you wish to accomplish if you aren't passionate and motivated. Pride gives us a sense of contentment and validation in our purpose. If you aren't proud of who you are and what you are doing in life, chances are that you operate on auto pilot. Sitting back comfortably each day as someone else (job, spouse, responsibilities) takes control of your life. You likely go to work 40-plus hours a week and do just enough to keep your bosses happy before rushing home to switch off in front of the TV as your hopes and dreams slowly slip away. At some point in our lives, we've all felt that overwhelming sense of dread that washes over us as soon as we open our eyes in the morning.

The apprehension and hesitation that begins to consume you as you prepare for yet another day at work. If what you do every day doesn't consume you and excite you, you are not living your purpose. Tall poppies ooze confidence and are passionate because they are proud of who they are and what they do. Though many have tried, pride is not something you can fake. Whenever you are feeling ashamed, hesitant or unsure on the inside, it will project on the outside. The key is to be authentic in all that you do as authenticity leads to success.

Project: Tall poppies know what they want and how they're going to get it. They wake up every day with a mission and a plan and more often than not go home each night with that mission accomplished. An important tool for achieving success is the ability to project. While many of us wish we could simply look into a crystal ball to predict the future, we can't. We can however use our inner intuition paired with logic and research to get the best results in anything we do. To project means to foresee, which in essence enables you to determine what is possible. You will need to do the groundwork necessary for each goal in order to be prepared to achieve them. When you do your research, you are able to make informed decisions. You will fail, but what matters is how well you succeed after that. Projection is a great tool for understanding the risks involved before you begin to live your purpose. There are many routes you can take on the road to success. Being informed enables you to pick the fastest route with the least amount of risks.

Plan: Projection is a great tool for planning but ultimately, what will best enable you to achieve your purpose is an in-depth plan. Who, what, how, why, where and when? These questions may seem like they're easy to answer but for some people, they're not. It's easy to image what kind of car you'll buy when you finally become a Hollywood actor, but without a plan in place this dream is just a fantasy. Living with intention means waking up everyday with your goals in mind and a burning desire to achieve them all that day.

Having structure and a plan creates focus and a visual map for achieving success. Every day should involve ticking off a checklist as you work through your plan. It's important that your plan is properly outlined and realistic. Planning to become a lawyer and not having a plan in place to go to law school is an unrealistic plan. Your plan should be thorough and logical to ensure that your time is used wisely. Checklists, diagrams, maps and notes are tools that assist with effective planning. Just as you would prepare for a uni exam, living with intention requires intense preparation and planning.

The above four P's are essential tools for living with intention, however gratitude is also needed. Every morning when I wake up, I express gratitude to the universe. Doing this helps remind me of everything that is going right in life. I find that when I take the time to say *"thank you,"* my day runs more smoothly and I am more efficient in everything that I do. At this stage, you should have a solid understanding of what exactly your life purpose is. Now it is time for you to do your part in making your dreams a reality. This requires a lot of patience.

"If you believe you've been called to do this, don't you ever give up. Don't you ever quit. Don't ever say it's not happening fast enough, you just keep doing it." - Cheryl Wood.

Patience and manifestation enabled me to achieve my dreams. When I first graduated from university, I was working in an entry-level job for one of Australia's biggest banks. I travelled two hours total to the office each day and worked 40-plus hours a week in a call centre role. The money was average and my work was tedious. The company itself had a great work culture but I was bored and overqualified for the job. I stayed in the role for two years which prompted criticism from my loved ones.

You have a degree, why aren't you using it?
You need a better job, you're too good for that.

Little did they know, I had a plan. At the time, the world was in the midst of a global financial crisis (GFC), so there were staffing freezes across the country. My plan was to save enough money to pursue my dreams of moving to New York and working in a journalism job that allowed me to travel. I found myself frustrated at times because even when I explained my plan, others couldn't understand my dream. The judgement turned from why are you working in such a basic job to why would you risk losing a secure job to pursue the unknown. The fact is judgement will always surround whatever it is you do. Although the judgement was disheartening, I learned to practice patience by visualising my own success whenever I felt like throwing in the towel. Eventually, when I made my big move the same people who criticised my dreams began asking how I did it.

Many people will give up if they don't see results right away. It's important to understand that dreams will often take time to manifest. During my career as an entertainment journalist in New York, it was my dream to work for one of the biggest media companies in the world. As the city was the media capital of the world, the job market was saturated. I lacked confidence and convinced myself that in order to have any chance in getting an interview, I'd have to apply for a role that I was overqualified for.

Because I believed it, that was the case. I applied for a traineeship program that would take place in London before my final placement. During my interview I spoke well, answered every question perfectly and left feeling excited. Much to my shock, I did not get the job. I had all the right experience and great enthusiasm. I could not for the life of me understand in that moment why this had happened. It's often said that sometimes the universe will say "no" to make room for something much greater in your life. Roughly six months after that disappointment, I examined the same company about an unrelated matter. After a brief email exchange, I was unofficially presented with an opportunity to join the company. The role would involve me taking on a leadership role, and I would be leading a small group of writers - including trainees from London. I couldn't believe my luck. I had been devastated after missing out on a traineeship and now, six months later, I would be leading them.

"Remember that sometimes not getting what you want is a wonderful stroke of luck." - Dalai Lama.

Living with intention requires you to function under a high level on consciousness both physically and emotionally. Once you understand how to do this, your mind, body and spirit will be in sync and enable you to tap into your higher power. The greatest power that one can acquire comes from within. When you truly have self-worth, life will naturally be lived more consciously. You begin to make better choices and happiness becomes a way of life. Waking up each day should be viewed as an opportunity to grow and live your best life.

You should wake up with intent and each move you make should be toward fulfilling your purpose and living the life of your dreams. Every single aspect of your life should in some way facilitate your dreams and draw you closer to achieving them. If there is something hindering your growth or deterring you from your purpose, it must go immediately. Whatever it is, if it does not advance your success or at the very least make you happy, it must be removed. There are two things to consider as you work towards living with intention, your emotional well-being and your physical well-being.

Emotional well-being: Happiness is a way of life. Intentional living is most effective when one is centred, which means being stress-free, happy and content. This means finding peace in all areas of life even though they may not all be perfect. Being centred does not mean being free of problems, it means finding tranquility despite your problems. It's having the ability to persevere and stay uplifted in the midst of adversity but also having the wisdom to stay humble and grounded during the highest of highs. Your goals and your success should always be the centre of your focus. There is no room for envy, judgement and cutting down others because each moment wasted worrying about another person is time taken away from fulfilling your purpose.

Physical well-being: Your health reflects your way of life. Therefore, a healthy diet and exercise should be a natural part of your daily routine. No one is born a healthy eater or an exercise enthusiast, people simply choose to live healthy lifestyles the same way others choose not to. What you put inside your body affects how you think and feel about yourself.

Any doctor will attest to the fact that choosing healthy options has tremendous effects on the body. For years, health experts have stressed the importance of healthy eating yet we're consuming junk food and other processed foods more than ever. It's not always easy to make healthy choices but it can be done with enough discipline. Change your thinking and eventually it becomes a habit. In addition to incorporating more fruit and vegetables into your diet, it's important that you make time to exercise regularly. Taking care of your body goes hand in hand living with intention. Neglecting your body and health shows a lack of discipline and lack of self-worth.

Take action:

Dream. Hope. Achieve.

Once you have both your emotional and physical well-being in check, living with intention becomes a breeze and eventually this is done subconsciously. Choosing a life of greatness is a choice, but not everyone understands this. Anyone who truly values their life knows that they deserve to be happy and live abundantly. When you know your value, you know what you deserve. Too many of us believe that we're not worthy of love and that we don't deserve happiness, but this is a lie.

We live in a world where telling people they're not worthy and not good enough can be lucrative business. Make it a daily habit to assure yourself that you are in fact worthy and deserving. Everyone is equal and no one is more or less deserving. The very best things in life are available to you and they are yours for the taking. You are ready for change and now is the time to start living your purpose. Your success and your happiness can help others by inspiring them to also pursue their dreams.

Living with intention is not easy, if it were everyone would do it. Living with intention requires constant focus and commitment. It's imperative that you stay on track and avoid doing the following:

Comparisons: This goes back to conformity and what we learn as kids in school. No life is the same, everyone comes from different walks so it's illogical to compare yourself with another person. Whether you perceive someone to be above you or beneath you, comparing yourself to another person is harmful because you are subconsciously relinquishing your inner power to that person. By comparing yourself to your neighbour you are giving them the control to dictate how you see yourself. Stay centred and always be inspired by the next person's success.

Self-doubt: That annoying little voice in the back of your head will no doubt grow louder as you advance towards enlightenment and as you begin to live your purpose. The key is learning to block it out because eventually, it disappears. One of the most common challenges that you will face as you begin to live a life of greatness is learning to believe that you are worthy of success. You may begin to doubt yourself and your hard-earned success. Ignore the voice, it's full of lies and doubt and serves you no purpose. When you do this, the transition from mediocrity to greatness becomes that much smoother.

Triggers: Once you've retrained your mind and mastered the art of positive thinking, you will at times find yourself going back to old habits (Chapter One). Whether this is toxic friends or negative thought patterns, familiarity will try and convince you that life was better when you were comfortable. No matter how rational your thoughts may seem, trust deep down that they are not. Your body and mind are simply craving what they used to know. Trust the decisions you made in Chapter One and embrace the changes. Do not second-guess yourself, stick with the process.

RECAP

Dream: Picture the life of your dreams. Does it make you feel passionate and excited? If not, you haven't yet discovered your purpose. Once you do, you will feel invigorated and like a new person. Think back to the goals you outlined in chapter's one and two. There should be an overwhelming sense of pride and contentment around your purpose. Consider the following: what is your legacy? What do you want to be remembered for? Who do you want to be remembered as? Will the dreams that you are working towards now leave you feeling honoured and proud 10 - 20 years from now? Never limit yourself and be persistent. If you truly want it, you can achieve it but you will need to have clarity and good intentions.

Hope: Living with intention requires a sense of hope. Consider your purpose. Why do you want to achieve it? How will achieving your goals elevate you on a personal level? Your dreams should always give you a renewed sense of hope about your life and the direction in which you are headed. Always stay focused on the prize while also being adaptable to change.

Achieve: All success requires maintenance so you make a conscious effort to improve your situation day in and day out. Do not stay stagnant, always strive to grow and build no matter how successful you become. Always remember where you came from and how hard you worked to get to get to the top. Success is temporary so be proactive and consistent in achieving new goals. Use your past struggles as a means for inspiration even after you've made it.

NOTES

CHAPTER SEVEN
Principle 1: Maintain success

Well done on reaching the final chapter. Your commitment to change is an indication that you are finally ready to live your best life. I trust that the knowledge in this book will greatly assist you on your journey. Before we explore how to maintain success, let's revisit some key points.

In Chapter One we defined envy as it relates to TPS. We also looked at its role in Aussie culture today and how it acts as a barrier between where you are and where you want to be. Feeling envious is not negative, in fact it's human nature. It's how you react to your emotions that counts. Tall poppies are not immune from feeling envy and jealousy, they've simply mastered the art of channelling their feelings. This can easily be done when you learn how to take control of your life (Chapter Four).

Your environment plays are big role in whether or not you allow emotions like envy to consume you. Misery loves company. Toxic energy breeds more of the same. Negative minds will attract like-minded people. Be sure to cleanse your environment of all sources of toxicity if you are serious about living your best life. Irrespective of what you were told growing up, it *is* all about you. Put yourself first and do whatever's in your best interest to be the best person you can be. For some this will mean taking a break from something or someone, for others this will mean cutting ties altogether. Regardless, you will need to make changes to get the most out of this process.

In Chapter Two we focused on the internal cleanse and retraining the mind. We learned that while obedience and conformity worked when we were children, it doesn't work today. There is power in your individuality, so it's time to embrace all the things that make you different. Standing out from the crowd is an opportunity to make a real impact. Learn to view yourself differently. Once you have a renewed sense of identity, you can begin renewing your mind, body and spirit. These are three separate aspects that makeup who were are, yet they are all related to one another. When they are in synch, magic happens.

Unlearning what you've known since you were a child might seem impossible, but with enough willpower and persistence — anything is possible. You were born to be different, you are destined to be happy and you will succeed. Learn to believe in your own greatness. At school we're taught to conform and if you weren't like everyone else you were deemed a rebel. This is a lie and must be unlearned. It's time to celebrate your unique talents and put them to use. You are worthy of success and it's your for the taking, it's simply up to you to pursue it.

Chapter Three analyses discovering your purpose. *Why are we here? What's the point of all of this? Who am I?* These are all common questions that many people will ask themselves throughout their life. Everyone is born with a purpose, it's up to us to figure out what that is. This will be harder for some than it is for others. Discovering your life purpose requires honesty, forgiveness and letting go of fear. You will first need to learn to be honest with yourself and your feelings. What makes you happy? What drives you? What are you most passionate about? These are just a few questions that when answered honestly can unlock dreams and lead you to a life of greatness.

Forgiveness means letting go of the past. We cannot plan ahead, when we're focused on what's behind us. Any past hurt, trauma and disappointments must be released. For most people, this is likely not something that will be done in one day. Blocking something out is one thing, but to really move on from pain healing is required. That could mean therapy, a long overdue conversation or a crying session.

Whatever it takes for you to fully heal must be done before you can finally achieve true happiness.

The number one reason that most people do not live their best lives is fear. The overwhelming doubt that comes over you when you dare to take a risk. For some people their fear of failure ultimately kills their dream. They would rather live a life of comfort because the thought of rejection and humiliation is simply too much. Over the past few decades, society has begun normalising fear. From seemingly never-ending terrorist attacks to health concerns, most of the information that we receive is a form of fear-mongering.

Many news organisations use scare tactics or clickbait to get your attention because fear breeds insecurity, which leads to dependency. Since the tragic events of 9/11, society has become obsessed with surveillance and understandably paranoid about national security. While the increased prioritisation of safety is warranted, the overwhelming sense of fear behind safety initiatives extends to other areas of life. We've become more suspicious of our neighbours, less trusting of the government and uncertain about the future. This uncertainty lowers confidence in ourselves and our abilities, which ultimately makes us less likely to take risks. The first step in releasing fear is to accept that failure is a reality and not the end of the world. Once you realise that the mere possibility of succeeding is far greater than the comfort of living a life of mediocrity, fear can no longer control your destiny.

In Chapter Four we explored different ways to take back your power. We learned about the need for focus and the importance of earning respect to be taken seriously. Most people don't realise that they're not in control of their lives. While it may appear as though they're in the driver's seat, others are actually in control. Every day that you spend working in a miserable job, you relinquish your power. Each minute that you spend thinking a negative thought, you relinquish power. Every time you waste energy trying to cut others down, you relinquish power. To be successful in any area of life, you must take charge of your entire life. This means regaining your power and channelling all energy into your purpose. There will always be distractions bills, children, relationships, car troubles — the key is staying focused.

You can't afford to be distracted because that causes a derailment on your journey. Your purpose should naturally be your priority and therefore always be at the centre of your focus. Staying focused shows genuine interest and passion, which means you are more inclined to be taken seriously by others. You cannot respect others if you don't respect yourself. The same rings true that if you don't respect yourself, no one will. Self-respect is developed once we know our value. If we don't believe in ourselves, chances are we won't see ourselves as valuable. When mind, body and spirit are in sync and you discover your true purpose, you will stop at nothing to achieve success. However, you need to have integrity to earn the respect of your peers. Many successful people have often failed because they lacked integrity. Whether it was illegal activity, dishonesty or a lapse in judgement, they lacked morals and subsequently failed. When you adhere to values and principles, you earn the respect of others, which makes it easier to achieve success.

In Chapter Five we explored learning to trust yourself. Your character determines whether you like yourself and subsequently, how capable you are of trusting yourself. The first step is to know yourself. Self-awareness is a fundamental tool that allows us to recognise our own presence in the world and the presence of others. Self-respect is developed through our morals and values and makes others more inclined to respect us. When we live with integrity, we live more consciously which enables us to take pride in our character. When you are willing to own your character by taking full responsibility for who you are, you learn to trust yourself.

In Chapter Six, we learned the importance of living with intention. This means waking up each day with a sense of hope and motivation to achieve your goals. When you operate in a zombie state, meaning you are constantly disconnected from life, you are never present. As best-selling author Eckhart Tolle explains in *The Power of Now - if you are not living in the now, you are living in the past or future* - which is unfulfilling and potentially destructive. Being present gives you a sense of awareness, which enables you to observe life as it happens and live with intent. Learning to set daily intentions, also helps us stay in the now. This means finding new ways to work towards your goals, for example: signing up for culinary classes to become a chef or putting aside money for that dream trip to Africa. While your goals are in the future, setting intentions is in the now/ present. Remember the four P's: Purpose, Pride, Project, Plan. Purpose is what you are passionate about. Pride is truly believing in your dreams and being motivated to achieve them. Project is researching and preparing for your own success. Plan is creating the most effective way to make your dreams a reality. Practicing gratitude for your life as it is helps manifest more greatness. To live with intent is to have clarity and purpose for your life.

The key to unlocking your purpose lies in your underlying intention: ego VS heart. Most people don't understand the difference between their ego and their heart. Ego refers to the self-serving aspects of your personality, while the heart relates to your highest self. When any action stems from the ego, it lacks substance and is done with the wrong intention. However, whenever an action comes from the heart, it is more likely to be sincere and done with the right intention.

Removing the ego leads to more authentic actions and ideas. To maintain success, you must never give up.

A friend of mine was a young married mother-of-two, with little to no money when she decided to take a huge life risk. She was fed-up with working a dead-end 9-5 job just to pay bills and decided to be her own boss. She was passionate about children and decided to open her very own childcare business. She had limited qualifications, limited funds and limited support but she felt called to do it. Her husband was understandably concerned, particularly because most small businesses most within their first year. However, she believed in her dream and her vision. For her, it was not just about financial freedom, it was about teaching, learning and actively helping raise the next generation.

The first month was great, the second was even better. She had done a great job networking and through word-of-mouth, she attracted new business. Money was flowing in, clients seemed happy and for the first time in her life - she felt content with her work. Although she was working longer hours, she felt a sense of freedom working for herself. One day, she had an unhappy client which threw her off completely. She was always someone who went above and beyond for anyone in her life - be in family, friends and clients. So the complaint was baffling. Unbeknownst to her, the client had a notoriously difficult personality and encountered problems everywhere she went. Although she would later discover that the client's complaint was unwarranted, at the time she took it personally.

She was unprepared in handling criticism, which led her to question herself. She began doubting her abilities as a business owner and even doubted the business itself and suddenly, business began to decline. Within a few months of that incident, she began experiencing financial woes and no longer enjoyed what she thought was her passion months prior. Her inability to thoroughly prepare herself to run a business led her to crumble at the first sight of trouble. When you fail to plan, you plan to fail. Fortunately in her case, the problems were temporary and she managed to regain her passion and confidence in the business. You will be criticised, attacked and judged throughout your journey to success, you simply must develop meaningful ways to help you overcome it. Learn to block out the noise and stay focused on your purpose in order to maintain success.

One of the biggest misconceptions about success as it relates to TPS is that to maintain success, it must be limited. That being "too successful" results in failure. This is a lie that will only lead to fear. To maintain success, you must own your failures and adapt to change. As previously mentioned, you will indeed fail at some point but it's how you rise from failure that matters. Just as you own your greatness, you need to own your failures and learn from them. What you don't acknowledge, you can't change so it's vital that you avoid repeating the same mistakes. There are two ways to do this: 1. Take responsibility for your life and 2. Be proactive.

Take responsibility: As noted in Chapter Four, to be successful you need to take charge of your life. That means owning your highs and lows. Too many people fall into the habit of blaming others when things don't work out. Whether it's a failed relationship, unsuccessful business or emotional struggles — you are responsible. We will often blame family, friends, colleagues, bosses or even strangers. This is a recipe for failure. By acknowledging your role in every difficult situation, you allow yourself to recognise and learn from your mistakes. The reason that you are not honouring your greatness is you. It's not because you have children to worry about or a job that takes up all your time. You are not living your best life because you don't believe you are worthy. As mentioned in Chapter Three, the first step towards achieving success is to believe and in order to maintain it - you must continue believing.

Be proactive: Life is constantly changing. Your tastes, interests, priorities and passions are constantly evolving. Another effective way to maintain success is to initiate change, this means taking risks. In Chapter Six, we looked at the four P's - one of which is Projection, which is foreseeing change and implementing it before it happens. Being proactive means being ahead of things, which requires extensive preparation and risk taking. For example, as society shifts towards more conscious living, we are seeing a growing need for environmentally friendly products. Being aware of trends in the marketplace and changing behavioural patterns enables you to make informed decisions about how to expand and effectively maintain your success.

One of my favourite quotes comes from Paulo Coelho's *The Alchemist* - *"never stop dreaming."* Without dreams, there is no hope and without hope life becomes pointless. By opening yourself up to endless possibilities, you allow yourself to stay hopeful and motivated. The key to maintaining success lies in maintaining the same level of enthusiasm that you had when you first realised your purpose. But as life changes, so do our passions. It is important you adapt to these changes so as to stay motivated.

Take action

Serve. Persevere. Thrive.

There are three key points in maintaining success: Serve, Persevere and Thrive. Each point requires self-understanding, self-acceptance and self-improvement. Once you achieve success, it is critical that you never become complacent. This means you should not be arrogant in your own success. Staying humble enables you to stay focused on your purpose.

Serve: It's important not to confuse your hobby with your purpose. While the line is often blurred, there are ways to distinguish both. Your hobby is something you do for yourself in your spare time whereas your purpose is something that serves yourself and others and requires full time attention. When you begin living out your purpose, you feel content and inspired. To maintain success, you should constantly feel this way. Serving others makes us feel valuable and accomplished, which gives us the fuel we need to stay passionate and driven.

Persevere: You will repeatedly fail. The secret to overcoming failure is to transform it into success. This is done by keeping your eye on the prize. Whenever you hear "no," remember every "yes" that brought you this far. Rejection is often perceived as failure, when in actuality it's purely rejection.

The difference between those who succeed and those who don't is usually perseverance. Tall poppies never give up. While rejection can be disheartening for some, others use it is motivation to work ever harder. When you accept failure as inevitable, you eliminate fear and become empowered.

Thrive: A wise person once said *"familiarity breeds complacency."* When we become comfortable in our own success or afraid of expanding, we set ourselves up for failure. It is important to challenge yourself to ensure that you are always reaching your highest potential. One way people fail is by falling into old habits. You cannot revert back to old thought patterns and destructive behaviour. The best way to do this is to withstand challenges through willpower. Allow yourself to feel all the lingering effects of failure when it happens. Embrace pain, humiliation, sadness, frustration and anger but then release those feelings. This allows us to build a mental shield between ourselves and failure so it never breaks us down. When you are unafraid of failure and committed to challenging yourself, you begin to thrive.

RECAP

Capping your success only leads to failure. When we limit our potential, we do ourselves a great disservice. While humility is essential in maintaining success, it is not the same as self-deprecation as TPS suggests. Suppressing your excellence and remaining stagnant may be well received by insecurity, but it ultimately undermines your own success. Maintaining success requires growth and expansion. Once you achieve your goals, the objective should be to get better and better. Just as a plant needs water to grow, your dreams need to be watered regularly. The best way to achieve growth is through learning. No matter how successful you are, there is always new information to be learned. Many people will achieve some form of success at some point in their lives but not everyone will know how to maintain it. The following are vital tools in maintaing a life of greatness.

Prioritise: Achieving success in any area of life should never make you complacent. It should inspire you to continue expanding. Too often, when a person reaches a goal they get tunnel vision. They become so focused on their current success that they fail to see anything beyond that point. This leads to complacency, distractions and eventually a loss of interest. Their purpose is no longer their priority and they soon find themselves back to square one: living life on autopilot and feeling unfulfilled. Your purpose should remain your top priority even after you achieve success. Never forget what drove you to begin with. And when you do achieve everything that you set out to, it's time to challenge yourself by creating meaningful new goals.

Discipline: Maintaining success requires great discipline because the moment you begin living your best life, a whole new world will open up to you. Resources, tools and other things you may never have had access to before, will suddenly be at your beck and call. The most common is money, which tends to flow in abundance for those living their best life. The trick is to practice discipline and not be distracted. Your desire for longterm success should be greater than shiny rewards. If at any point your focus shifts from achieving your purpose to something else, then you have not yet discovered your true purpose. Practice discipline by staying focused on your longterm goals and resisting the temptation to get swept up in temporary success.

Patience: Expanding on your success can take time, so it's important to stay grounded and patient while you wait. Too often, people expect to be successful at a more rapid pace the second time around - which is flawed thinking. Success in general is never guaranteed, it's your hope and belief that determines your likelihood of achievement. When you are truly passionate about your cause, career, business etc, time simply does not apply. You subconsciously agree to pursue your purpose until you reach success. But even at that point, the focus should automatically shift to maintaining it.

NOTES

EPILOGUE

I wrote this book to inspire, motivate and awaken people. TPS is not a new concept and in fact, has been embodied in Aussie culture since as early as the 19th century. However, what is new is the realisation that it is detrimental to society. Everyone from our youth to veterans should be encouraged to achieve their full potential, yet instead they are made to suppress their abilities and strive for mediocrity. No matter how talented they may be, most would prefer to ignore their own greatness to be liked. Those who *do* find the courage to stand out from the crowd and embrace their talents are attacked, resented and cut down by others. When deemed to be "too successful" by others, they are often mocked and disregarded. I first realised how prevalent TPS is in Australia after living in the US for six years. There, encouragement is ingrained at a young age. People are encouraged and supported early on by teachers, parents and their peers to embrace their talents and strive for excellence.

However, in Australia, our young people are taught to conform and "stay grounded." They learn early on that their talents should never be touted because it makes those around them feel small. Remember the conditioning from when you were a child (Chapter Two): school-work-house-marriage-kids-retirement. This model is incompatible with modern society yet there's still an expectation that it will be followed.

In 2012, Doron Ben-Meir, CEO of government organisation Commercialisation Australia, told *The Sydney Morning Herald* that it's time for Australia to "grow up."

"We still do have a cultural problem with success and failure that we need to address and we need to start admiring our successful entrepreneurs as much as we admire our successful footballers and cricketers and tennis players.

I think culturally we gotta grow up and realise that we gotta start telling people how good we are and not expecting people to notice it, despite our humility ... culturally we've gotta get more comfortable with that and not try to cut people down."

The key to overcoming TPS is to encourage young people early on to pursue a life of greatness. Too many young people grow up believing that success is not attainable

(Chapter Three). Many dream about success but feel an overwhelming sense of hopelessness in their ability to make it happen. This usually continues into adulthood and will manifest throughout their lives. When you grow up thinking you can't, you won't. When you grow up believing you can, you will. The same applies to adults. Your mindset dictates your life situation. The good news is that it's never too late to change. Just because you grew up believing a lie, doesn't mean it has to continue. The only challenge is that as you get older, it becomes harder to change your mindset — but never impossible.

The best way to begin change is to take a close look at the internal and external factors blocking your success (Chapter Two and three). You will never solve problems with the same mindset that created them. Drastic change requires drastic decisions. Another key to overcoming TPS is to learn to block out criticism. When it comes to your success, your voice is the only one that truly matters. What others think, feel, like and dislike is not your concern. Your priority and focus is owning your greatness and living abundantly.

TPS should never discourage you from living a life of greatness. It's never easy to break-free from what's considered to be normal, but it's necessary if you are serious about achieving success. The internal and external cleanse help prepare you for the life you want to live. From bad people to bad habits, you can't afford to have distractions so all sources of toxicity must go. Whether these changes are permanent or temporary is up to you. However, temporary fixes usually result in temporary success. If your goal is to achieve short-term success, then temporary is the way to go. However, if like most people you want meaningful change in your life and longterm success then permanent is a better option.

We are all born with a purpose. This should be seen as your automatic license to be successful and live in abundance. The problem is that most people are yet to discover what their purpose is. The key is to really understand yourself and what you are passionate about in life. Spend time getting to know yourself (Chapter Five) and eventually, this will lead you to your purpose. You will know you have discovered your purpose by the way your heart responds. If you become completely consumed and if it gives you a sense of fulfilment deep within, you are on the right path.

But figuring out your purpose is only the beginning. The most difficult part is finding the courage to pursue it. Too many of us block our own success by overthinking and making excuses. We procrastinate because subconsciously we fear our own success. It may sound illogical but it's true, particularly when you don't believe you are worthy of success. Once you begin to trust yourself and believe in your purpose, you will naturally start to become serious about making your dreams a reality. Another important key to remember is the need to be fearless.

New York City is filled with some of the most accomplished people in the world. Many of the most prominent lawyers, doctors, bankers, moguls and tycoons reside in Manhattan. Living there for six years and personally interacting with these people through work led me to observe common traits they all share. These traits helped them and many others find the courage to live a life of greatness. They are ambitious, persistent and fearless. They know exactly what they want and will often stop at nothing to get it. Nothing gets in their way of achieving their goals. They do not allow people, emotions or bad situations to prevent their success. Most telling is that TPS does not exist in the United States. There, the achievements of others are recognised and celebrated. Ambition and creativity are encouraged from a very young age and this overall positive energy becomes contagious.

With that said, many successful people continue to thrive in Australia despite TPS. Stars like Melissa George and Rebel Wilson are prime examples of how it is still possible to thrive even when others try to cut you down. By following each of the seven principles in this book, you too can live your best life. Eradicating TPS would simply make it easier to achieve success and live a life of abundance. Instead of tearing down others, the goal should be to support and encourage those who dare to dream.

Alan Noble, Engineering Director at Google Australia, said extreme humility may *"actually hinder us."*

"Probably the one thing that would help more than anything else is visible success. There's nothing like success to foster success, we need to really shout out about our success stories and we tend to be probably a little bit too modest about our success. We've had some fantastic entrepreneurial success stories and yet most Australians would never have heard of them."

It is indeed possible to be both successful and humble. There are common misconceptions that they're mutually exclusive, just as some people believe success and arrogance go hand-in-hand. This flawed thinking has been ingrained in Aussie culture for decades and has proven to be destructive. The narrative must change in order to finally be free of ancient ideologies. Success can no longer be seen as unattainable and reserved only for a select few. Everyone from children to the elderly should live by the belief that anything in life is possible if you are willing to honour your true potential. Success is a fundamental birth right because after all, we are all born tall poppies.

A huge thanks to you.

I'm happy that you picked up this book. May it uplift, motivate and inspire you to live the life that you truly deserve.

Cheers to your success!
Love Mibengé

Printed in Great Britain
by Amazon